SOLZHENITSYN

SOLZHENITSYN

Georg Lukács

TRANSLATED FROM THE GERMAN BY
William David Graf

London
MERLIN PRESS

© Copyright 1969 by Hermann Luchterhand GmbH,
Neuwied & Berlin

Translation copyright The Merlin Press, 1970
First published in England by The Merlin Press,
11 Fitzroy Square, London, W.1.

Printed in Great Britain by Bristol Typesetting Co. Ltd.
Barton Manor, St. Philips, Bristol

Contents

I. Solzhenitsyn:

One Day in the Life of Ivan Denisovich

I.

THE AESTHETIC relationship between the novella and the novel has often been examined. Much less has been said about their historical connection and their interrelationship throughout the course of literary development. Yet here a most interesting and instructive problem is at hand, one which casts a particularly discerning light on the present-day situation. I am thinking of the fact that the novella frequently appears either as a precursor to a conquest of reality by the great epic and dramatic forms, or as a rearguard, a termination at the end of a period; that is, it appears either in the phase of a Not-Yet (*Nochnicht*) in the artistically universal mastery of the given social world, or in the phase of the No-Longer (*Nichtmehr*).

From this viewpoint, Boccaccio and the Italian novella appear as forerunners of the modern bourgeois novel. They depict the world in an era in which bourgeois forms of life were advancing victoriously and were increasingly beginning to destroy the medieval forms in the most diverse areas of life, and to replace these with their own forms. In this world, however, there could not yet be a totality of objects, nor could there be a totality of human relations and behaviour as interpreted by bourgeois society. On the other hand, Maupassant's novella appears as a kind of *Abgesang** of that world whose origin Balzac and Stendhal have depicted and whose extremely

*The third and last section of the strophe in the *Meistergesang* (of the *Meistersinger*)—*Trans.*

7

problematical consummation Flaubert and Zola have portrayed.

Such an historical connection can arise only on the foundation of peculiarities of genre. We have already pointed out that the totality of objects is the characteristic trait of the extensive universality of the novel; the totality of the drama has a different content and structure, but both aim at a comprehensive entirety of the activity depicted, and in both a manifold human pro and contra *vis à vis* the central questions of the era results in a totality of types which, contrasting and complementing each other, occupy the appropriate places in the progression of time. By contrast, the novella is based on a single situation and—on the level of plot and characters—remains there. It does not claim to shape the whole of social reality, nor even to depict that whole as it appears from the vantage point of a fundamental and topical problem. Its truth rests on the fact that an individual situation—usually an extreme one—is possible in a certain society at a certain level of development, and, just because it is possible, is characteristic of this society and this level. For this reason the novella can omit the social genesis of the characters, their relationships, the situations in which they act. Also for this reason, it needs no agencies to set these situations in motion and can forgo concrete perspectives. This peculiarity of the novella, which to be sure permits an infinite internal variety from Boccaccio to Chekhov, enables it to appear historically both as a forerunner and rearguard of the great forms; it can be the artistic representative of the Not-Yet or of the No-Longer, of a totality which can be portrayed.

Naturally we do not aspire to explain, nor even to suggest this historical dialectic here. However, to prevent any misunderstanding it must be said that the alternatives of Not-Yet and No-Longer here described, which are extremely important for the following reflections, by no means exhaust the historical connections between the novel and the novella. There is a great number of others which we shall tacitly pass over this time. Just to suggest the diversity of the connections possible here, we might mention Gottfried Keller. *Green Henry* had to leave the Switzerland of the young Keller in order to develop into a total novel. In the cycle *The People of Seldwyla*, the individual novellas, contrasting and complementing each other, produce a view of totality not portrayable in a novel. And the homeland, which has become capitalist, cannot, according to Keller's vision of man, produce a rich and effortlessly organized totality. But the "epigrammatical" novellas, considered as stories-within-stories carrying on controversies with each other, are able to present the ups and downs, the pros and cons of the development of a couple maturing to a genuine love. The immediate substance of the world accessible to Keller would have been incapable of this in a centralized novel. We find here, then, a unique interweaving of the Not-Yet and the No-Longer, which admittedly does not do away radically with the above-mentioned historical connection between the novel and novella, but which can by no means be directly classified within it. And literary history frequently demonstrates quite different interrelations which we cannot enter into here.

With this reservation, one can say of contemporary and near-contemporary fiction that it often withdraws from the novel into the novella in its attempt to provide proof of man's moral stature. I am referring to masterworks such as Conrad's *Typhoon* or *The Shadow Line* and Hemingway's *The Old Man and the Sea*. The withdrawal is already evident in the fact that the social basis, the social milieu of the novel disappears, and the central figure must hold his own against a pure natural occurrence. This duel in which the lonely hero left to his own devices struggles against nature, say against a storm or calm, can even end with the victory of man, as in Conrad; but even when it ends in defeat, as in Hemingway, the moral qualities of its heroes are the essential content of the novella. The contrast with the novels of these writers (and not only with theirs) is blatant: the social relationships devour, crush, mutilate, falsify, etc. the characters. It appears that there is no effective counter-force, not even one condemned to a tragic fall, to be found in this milieu. And since significant writers cannot possibly forgo all human integrity and inner greatness, novellas of the type just mentioned occur in their works as a rearguard action in their struggles for the deliverance of man.

In Soviet literature too, the forces of progress are concentrated—apart from lyric poetry—around the novella. Solzhenitsyn is surely not the only, but as far as we know *the* one who has succeeded in really breaking through the ideological bulwarks of the Stalinist tradition. It is the task of the following exposition to show that for Solzhenitsyn—and for those striving in a similar direction—it is a question of a beginning, an exploration of the new reality, and not, as in the works of the important bourgeois writers mentioned, the conclusion of a period.

2.

The central problem of socialist realism today is to come to terms critically with the Stalin era. Naturally this is the major task of all socialist ideology. Here I will confine myself to the field of literature. If socialist realism—which in consequence of the Stalinist period became at times a disdainful term of abuse, even in the socialist countries—desires to regain the level it had reached in the nineteen-twenties, then it must rediscover the way to depict contemporary man as he actually is. However, this way necessarily leads through a faithful portrayal of the Stalinist decades with all their inhumanities. Against this, the sectarian bureaucrats raise the objection that one should not rake up the past, but only describe the present. The past is said to be done, already completely outmoded, vanished from the present. Such a claim is not only untrue—the way in which it is presented demonstrates the still extremely influential presence of the Stalinist cultural bureaucracy—but it is also completely meaningless. When Balzac or Stendhal depicted the period of Bourbon restoration, they knew that they were portraying characters, the majority of whom had been shaped by the revolution, by Thermidor and its consequences, by the Empire. Julien Sorel or Père Goriot would be shadowy and elusive figures if only their momentary existences in the restoration had been depicted, and not their fates, their developments, their pasts. This is also true of the creative period of socialist realism. The main figures in Sholokhov, A. Tolstoy, the young Fadeyev, etc. originate in Czarist Russia; no one could understand their actions in the civil war without having first experienced how they arrived, from the pre-war era via the experiences of the imperialist war and the downfall of the Provisional Government, at their positions; and—above all—no one could comprehend just what their position is.

Few who today are active in the world of socialism have not in some way experienced the Stalinist period; there are few whose present intellectual, moral and political physiognomy has not been formed by the experience of this era. The notion of "the people" that is said to have developed in a socialist way and constructed socialism "unaffected" by the excesses of the "personality cult" is not even an untruthful wish-fulfilment; precisely those who proclaim it and operate with it know best—from experience—that the Stalinist system of rule had penetrated into all facets of everyday life, and that only in the remote villages were its effects not felt so strongly. Stated thus, this sounds like a generality. It was, however, manifest in different people in different ways, and individual reactions exhibit a seemingly infinite variety of attitudes. The alternatives posed by many Western ideol-

ogists, e.g. Molotov *versus* Koestler, are only more remote
from reality and a degree more stupid than the bureaucratic
view described above.

Should the latter view in fact become the criterion of
literature, we should find ourselves facing a straightforward
continuation of the "illustrating literature" of the Stalin era.
This was a crude manipulation of the present: it originated
not in the dialectic between the past and realistic aims for
the future, or in the actions of real human beings, but rather
was always determined in form and content by the momentary
resolutions of the apparatus. Since "illustrating literature" did
not grow out of life but rather originated in commentaries
to resolutions, the marionettes contrived for this purpose
must not and could not have a past like real human beings.
Instead they had mere "cadre papers" (personality tests) which
were filled in according to whether it was desired to regard
them as "positive heroes" or as "parasites".

The crude manipulation of the past is only one aspect of
the crude overall manipulations of the figures, situations,
fates, perspectives, etc. in the works of "illustrating literature".
For this reason the meaningless directive referred to above
is only an "up to date" and consistent continuation of the
Stalin-Zhdanov policy toward literature, a newly-discovered
hindrance to the regeneration of socialist realism—to its re-
gaining the capacity to describe genuine types of a period
who comment in their own individual ways on the great
and minor problems of their time, problems arising from the
necessity of their own lives. Since in the final analysis their
individuality is socio-historically conditioned, it is precisely
in this respect that the past-present perspective of the future
is most clearly expressed. The relationship between man and
society, as represented within a single personality, is most
concretely illustrated by showing the development of that
personality through his experiences, in the past. For, what
from an historical point of view is an identical past, obtains

a varied shape in each human life: the same events are experienced in different ways by human beings of different ages, etc. However, any given event has extraordinarily different effects on human beings and depending on whether it is near or far, central or peripheral, to say nothing of the sheer fortuitousness of individual mediating factors, it opens up a wide spectrum of human responses. And when confronted with such events, no man remains really emotionally passive. Man is always placed before alternatives—the choice can lead from resistance to compromise (be it intelligent or stupid, right or wrong), to collapse, to capitulation.

It is, however, never a question of mere isolated occurrences and reactions to events, but of the interconnections between these, and the earlier reactions are always a not unimportant factor in the later ones. Without uncovering the past, then, there is no discovery of the present. Solzhenitsyn's *One Day in the Life of Ivan Denisovich* is a significant overture to this process of literary rediscovery of the self in the socialist present.

The point here is not—at least not primarily—the horrors of the Stalin era, of the concentration camps, etc. This theme has existed for some time in Western literature. Moreover, since the XXth Congress placed a critique of the Stalinist period on its agenda, these horrors have lost their initial shock effect, above all in the socialist countries. Solzhenitsyn's achievement consists in the literary transformation of an uneventful day in a typical camp into a symbol of a past which has not yet been overcome, nor has it been portrayed artistically. Although the camps epitomize one extreme of the Stalin era, the author has made his skilful grey monochrome of camp life into a symbol of everyday life under Stalin. He was successful in this precisely because he posed the artistic question: what demands has this era made on man? Who has proved himself as a human being? Who has salvaged his human dignity and integrity? Who has held his own—and how? Who has retained his essential humanity? Where was this humanity twisted, broken, destroyed? His rigorous limitation to the immediate camp life permits Solzhenitsyn to pose the question simultaneously in quite general and quite concrete terms. The constantly changing political and social alternatives which life places before free human beings are in the nature of the case eliminated, but resistance or collapse are treated so directly in terms of concrete being or non-being of living people that every solitary decision is raised to the level of a true-to-life generalization and typification.

The entire composition, the details of which we will discuss later, serves this purpose. The slice of everyday camp life already described, as the central figure stresses at the end, presents a "good" day in camp life. And in fact nothing unusual, no special atrocity occurs on that day. We see the normal order of the camp and its inmates' typical reactions based on that order. In this way the typical problems can be sketched firmly, and it is left to the reader's imagination to visualize the effects on the characters of even greater tribulations. This almost ascetic concentration on essentials is matched exactly by the extreme economy of presentation. Of the outer world only the elements indispensable for their effect on the inner working of man are shown; of the emotional world of man only those reactions which are directly connected with their human substance in immediately comprehensible ways—and he is most sparing even with these. Thus this work—which is not even symbolically conceived— can exert a strong symbolic effect; thus the problems of everyday life in the Stalinist world—even though they have nothing immediately in common with camp life—are commented on implicitly in this description.

Even this extremely abstract synopsis of Solzhenitsyn's work shows that stylistically it is a story, a novella, and not a novel (however short), despite his efforts to achieve the greatest possible completeness and a mutual complementing

14

of types and fates through concrete description. Solzhenitsyn consciously avoids any perspective. Camp life is represented as a permanent condition; the very few allusions to the expiration of individual terms are kept extremely vague—and the dissolution of the camp does not even appear in daydreams. In the case of the central figure, it is merely stressed that his home has changed very much in the meanwhile, and that he can by no means return to the familiar old world; this too increases the seclusion of the camp. Thus the future is heavily veiled in all directions. What is foreseeable are similar days, better or worse, but not radically different. The past is likewise represented with economy. A few hints at how certain individuals have come into the camp reveal, precisely in their impartial and laconic paucity of words, the arbitrariness of the legal and administrative, military and civilian sentences. Not a word is said about the basic political questions, for example the Great Trials; they have been swallowed up into an obscure past. Even the personal injustice of deportation, which is touched on only in individual cases, is not criticized directly, but rather appears as a hard fact, a necessarily accepted presupposition of this camp existence. Everything which could and should become the task of the great novels and dramas of the future is consciously eliminated here. In this we may see a formal, but purely formal—stylistic similarity to the significant novellas mentioned earlier. This does not mean a retreat from the great forms as it did then, but rather an initial exploration of a reality in the search for the great forms appropriate to it.

The world of socialism today stands on the eve of a renaissance of Marxism, a renaissance whose task it will be not only to eliminate Stalinist distortions and point to the way forward, but above all adequately to encompass the new facts of reality with the old-new methods of genuine Marxism. In literature, socialist realism faces a similar task. The continuation of that which in the Stalin era was praised and distinguished as socialist realism would be futile. I believe, however, that it is also wrong to attempt to give socialist realism a premature burial by re-christening everything that has arrived in Western Europe since expressionism and futurism as realism and dropping the attribute "socialist". If socialist writers were to reflect upon their task, if they were again to feel an artistic responsibility towards the great problems of the present, powerful forces could be unleashed leading in the direction of relevant socialist literature. In this process of transformation and renewal, which signifies an abrupt departure from the socialist realism of the Stalin era, the role of landmark on the road to the future falls to Solzhenitsyn's story.

Such harbingers of a literary springtime can, of course, achieve historical importance as heralds of an era without their works having any special artistic merit. Lillo and after him Diderot as the first discoverers of the bourgeois drama are obvious examples. However, Solzhenitsyn's historical position is a different one. When Diderot theoretically placed social conditions at the centre of a dramaturgical interest, he opened up an important thematic area for tragedy; his pioneering role is not invalidated by the realization of the mediocrity of his dramas, but is merely restricted to an abstract recognition of his topics. However, by portraying life in concentration camps, Solzhenitsyn has not made a comparable contribution to the theme of literature. On the contrary, his mode of writing, with its concern for the quotidian reality of the Stalinist era and its human alternatives breaks new ground in its treatment of the problems of survival or going under. The concentration camp is a symbol of everyday Stalinist life, and Solzhenitsyn's achievement is to make the representation of camp life itself a mere episode in the universality in which everything of significance for individual and social *praxis* in the present will be represented as the indispensable prelude to that present.

3.

Readers have felt this one day of Ivan Denisovich to be a symbol of the Stalin era. Yet there is not a trace of symbolism in Solzhenitsyn's descriptive method. He presents a genuine, realistic slice of life in which no single aspect obtrudes itself simply for effect or exaggerated effect or for any symbolic motive. To be sure, the typical fate, the typical behaviour of millions is concentrated into this slice. This straightforward fidelity to nature in Solzhenitsyn's work has nothing whatever in common with naturalism—either with direct naturalism or the kind brought about with technical refinement. Contemporary discussions of realism, and above all of socialist realism, pass heedlessly over the real basic question, not least because they lose sight of the contrast between realism and naturalism. In the "illustrating literature" of the Stalin era, an official naturalism, combined with an equally official, so-called revolutionary romanticism, was substituted for realism. Admittedly naturalism in the nineteen-thirties was contrasted with realism in an abstractly theoretical way. But only abstractly, and this abstraction could have been made concrete only through an opposition to the "illustrating literature", because in practice the manipulators of literature dismissed as naturalist those and only those facts which were in conflict with official objectives; in line with this practice, naturalism could be overcome only if the writer selected for his representation exclusively those facts which directly or indirectly justified the directives which the work concerned was intended to illustrate. Typification thus became a purely political category. Independently of the dialectic inherent in the characters and their human essence, a positive or negative value judgement of the writer's attitude, which appeared favourable or unfavourable to the execution of the resolution concerned, was evident in typification. Now this policy gave rise to an extremely artificial construction of plots and characters, a construction which was necessarily naturalistic to some degree, since one characteristic of this descriptive method was that the details it presented were not necessarily interconnected nor linked organically with the active characters, their fates, etc. They remain pale, abstract or excessively concrete, according to the individual writer, but are never combined into an organic unity with the creative material, since in essence they are brought into it from without. I call attention to the scholastic debates concerning the extent to which a positive hero can have or ought to have negative traits. Implicit in this controversy is a denial of the fact that in literature the concrete and individual character is primary—the beginning and end of the creative process. Here characters and fates can and ought to be manipulated at will. Should it happen, as many now wish, that modern Western descriptive methods replace outmoded socialist realism, then the basic naturalist character of the dominant currents in modern literature would be generally neglected in both camps. I have repeatedly called attention, in various contexts, to the fact that the various "isms", which in their time replaced naturalism proper, have left intact this lack of inner cohesion, this compositional incoherence in naturalism, this separation of the immediate unity of substance and appearance. In principle, the overcoming of the main feature of naturalism, namely its adherence to immediate observations, or its replacement with one-sidedly objective or one-sidedly subjective projections, does not affect this basic problem of naturalism at all. We are now speaking of general literary practice, and not of significant exceptional achievements. Gerhard Hauptmann is not a naturalist in an aesthetic sense in his *The Weavers* or *Beaver Coat*, whereas the great mass of expressionists, surrealists, etc. have never overcome naturalism. Seen from this vantage point, it is thus easy to understand why a great part of the opposition to the socialist realism of the Stalin era seeks out and believes to have found its refuge in modern literature. For this transition can be accomplished on the level of a purely subjectivist spontaneity without radically disturbing the writer's relationship to social reality, without going beyond his fundamental naturalist attitude, without his living through and thinking out the great contemporary problems. This does not even necessitate a break with "illustrating literature"; already in the nineteen-thirties there were novels about industrialization, consistent with the party line, which employed all the achievements of expressionism, the "new objectivity" or montage, but which differed only in external technique from the average officially approved production of this time. There are indications that this could repeat itself even today; it must be remarked of course that a purely subjective and persistent negation has for some time not signified an imaginative and artistic conquest of the aerarian Yes.

Solzhenitsyn's tale stands in marked contrast to all the trends within naturalism. We have already discussed the extreme economy of his descriptive method. The consequence of this in his work is that his details are always highly significant. As in every genuine work of art, the particular shade of meaning originates in the singularity of the material itself. We are in a concentration camp: each morsel of bread, each rag, every scrap of stone or metal that can be used as a tool serves to prolong life; but to take along something of this nature in marching out to work or to conceal it somewhere involves a risk of discovery, of confiscation, indeed of solitary confinement; each facial expression and each gesture by a superior requires an immediate and specific reaction which, if not correct can bring disaster in its wake; on the other hand there are situations, e.g. occasionally during the dispensing of meals, in which resolute action at the right time can earn a double portion. According to Hegel, the epic greatness of the Homeric poems rests in great measure on the significance attached to the impressive and accurate description of eating, drinking, sleeping, physical work, etc. In everyday bourgeois life these functions largely lose this specific importance, and only the very greatest, such as Tolstoy, are able to reproduce these complicated mediations. (Naturally such comparisons serve only to illuminate the artistic problems at hand, and ought by no means to be understood as value judgements.)

The detail in Solzhenitsyn's work has a peculiar function which grows out of the nature of his material: it renders conspicuous the suffocating constriction of everyday camp life, its monotony shot through with peril, the never-resting capillary movements, barely sufficient for the preservation of life. Every detail presents an alternative between survival and succumbing, every object is a trigger of a salutary or destructive fate. In this way the adventitious existence of individual objects is inseparably and visibly bound up with the curves of individual fates. Thus the concentrated totality of camp life is evoked with the very greatest economy, the sum and system of this mean, threadbare reality results in a humanly significant symbolic totality which illuminates an important aspect of human life.

On this experimental basis Solzhenitsyn builds a particular form of the novella whose parallels and contrasts with the above-mentioned great modern novellas of the bourgeois world cast light on the historical situation of both. In both groups man struggles against an all-powerful and hostile environment whose cruelty and inhumanity reveal its naturelike essence. In Conrad or Hemingway, this hostile environment is actually nature. (Storm or calm in Conrad; but even where strictly human destinies are at work, as in *The End of the Tether*, growing blind—the cruelty of his own biological nature—is what the old captain has to contend with.) The social nature of human relationships is thrust into the background and often pales to the point of disappearing altogether. Man is set against nature itself; either he must stand up to it relying on his own strength or he must perish. For this reason, every detail of this duel is important, objectively fateful and subjectively offering an alternative between survival and doom. However, since man and nature are immediately set against each other, the pictures of nature can take on an Homeric breadth without their fatal intensity being weakened, because in this way the fateful relation to the actor is again and again compressed into significant decisions. But for this very reason the pre-eminently social relationships among the characters would fade away, indeed disappear, when such novellas appear at the end of a literary development.

In Solzhenitsyn's works too, the totality portrayed has nature-like features. It simply exists, as a *factum brutum*, without a visible genesis in the movements of human life, without further developing into another form of social existence. But it is always and everywhere a "second nature", a social complex. However "natural", inexorable, cruel, senseless, inhuman its effects may appear, they *are* consequences of human acts, and a person defending himself against them must behave quite differently toward them than toward real nature. Hemingway's old fisherman can even feel sympathy and admiration for the powerful fish whose stubborn resistance almost destroys him.

This is impossible *vis à vis* the representatives of the "second nature". Solzhenitsyn does not avoid a clear-cut expression of inner resistance, but this is contained implicitly in every spare expression and gesture. For the natural physical expressions of life, such as cold, hunger and the like, in the last analysis are mediated by the relations of man to man. Survival or the failure to survive are also seen in directly social terms; even if this is never openly stated, they refer to a future real life, to a life in freedom among other free men. Of course contained in this is also a "nature-like" element of immediate physical survival or immediate physical destruction, but the dominant factor is objectively the social one. For nature is really independent of us humans; it can be subordinated to practical human knowledge, but its essence is necessarily immutable. However natural the "second nature" may appear at first sight, it is a structure of human relations, our own creation. Therefore, the ultimate, healthy attitude toward it is a desire to change, improve, make human. The truth of the details too, their substance, their external appearance, their interaction, their combinations, etc. are always of a social character, even when their genesis does not appear directly as social. Here again Solzhenitsyn austerely refrains from any expression of opinion. However, precisely the objectivity of his descriptive method, the "natural" cruelty and inhumanity of a social-human institution, result in a more devastating judgement than any lofty declamation would be able to pronounce. And similarly, the austere abstinence from any perspective itself contains a concealed perspective. Without it being stated, every proving of oneself, and every failure to prove oneself point to the future normal mode of human relations; they are—implicitly—preludes to a real future life among men. This slice of life is, therefore, not an end but a social prelude to the future. (In a purely individual sense, the struggle against real nature can also be a human education, as in Conrad's *The Shadow Line*, only in a strictly individual way. The captain's victory in *Typhoon* is, as Conrad stresses, an interesting episode without consequences.)

This leads back to the symbolic effect of Solzhenitsyn's story: it results, implicitly, in a concentrated prelude to the approaching artistic debate with the Stalinist period in which such slices of life did in fact symbolize everyday reality. This was a prelude to the portrayal of the present, of the world of the people who—directly or indirectly, actively or passively, strengthened or broken—have passed through this "school", and whose present-day lives and activities were formed in it. Herein lies the paradoxical character of Solzhenitsyn's literary position. His laconic expression, his refraining from any allusion that would point beyond the immediacy of camp life nevertheless sketches in the central human and moral problems without which contemporary man would be objectively impossible and subjectively incomprehensible. Precisely in its concentrated, economical reserve, this immediate, extremely limited slice of life is an overture to the great literature of the future.

Solzhenitsyn's other known novellas do not have the same degree of symbolic comprehensiveness. But perhaps for this very reason his exploration of the past in order to find a way of comprehending the present is, as we will see, all the more clearly manifest. This view of the present is least visible in the fine novella *Matriona's House*. In it Solzhenitsyn, like some of his contemporaries, depicts life in a remote village where the people and ways of life are very little influenced by socialism and its Stalinist form. (The existence of such possibilities is not unimportant for the overall picture of the present, but it is by no mean central.) It is a portrait of an old woman who has experienced and suffered a great deal. who was often deceived and always exploited, and whose deep inner goodness and serenity nothing could shake. Here we have the example of a character whose humanity nothing was able to break or mar; a portrait in the spirit of the great Russian realist tradition. In Solzhenitsyn's works, however, only the tradition in general is noticeable, and not the stylistic continuation of any single master. This connection with the best Russian tradition is similarly visible in his other novellas. Thus the composition of *One Day in the Life of Ivan D.* is constructed upon the moral similarities and contrasts of a number of main figures. In contrast to the clever, tactically adroit, rustic main character who never surrenders his human dignity, there is on the one hand the passionate ex-frigate captain who risks his existence because he cannot let an indignity pass without protest, and on the other the sly brigade leader who skilfully represents the interests of his co-workers before the authorities but who at the same time uses these co-workers to enhance his own—relatively privileged—position.

More dynamic and much more closely connected with the problematics of the Stalin era is the novella, *An Incident at the Kretchetovka Station*, which focuses on the social and moral aspects of the time of crisis, or "vigilance". In a twofold dialectical process it shows how the routine of Stalinist slogans distorts all genuine problems of life. Here too there is—again in the true manner of the novella—only a unique, individual conflict and its immediate solution without as much as a hint of how the decision taken influences the lives and further development up to the present of those concerned. However, the conflict is constituted in such a way that the tension created by it makes waves which spill over the actual bounds of the novella. The alternative to "vigilance" and the pressure towards "vigilance", was not only a burning problem of those lost days; their after-effects, the forces that shaped the moral personalities of many people, are still active today. The story of the camp could bravely but in the spirit of resignation forgo any perspective, any mention of the present not only in the description itself but also in the complementary imagination of the informed reader; but at the conclusion of this work we are faced with the question, posed with deliberate, painful candour: how will the enthusiastic young officer come to terms with this experience? What kind of a man is he—and many people like him—for having been the perpetrator of such a deed?

The characteristic of the novella, which artistically is just as true to form as the other type, appears to be intensified in *For the Good of the Cause*, Solzhenitsyn's latest work, which aroused great enthusiasm and violent rejection in Soviet literature. Here the gauntlet thrown down by the sectarians before the friends of progressive literature—namely the claim that the enthusiasm of the masses for reconstruction work during the era of the "personality cult" should be described "independently" of that cult—is boldly taken up. It concerns the building of a technical school in a provincial town; the old premises are completely inadequate, the pupils cannot be accommodated, and the authorities are bureaucratically delaying the necessary new buildings. Here however, is a genuine collective of teachers and pupils bound by mutual trust, indeed love; during the holidays they voluntarily undertake the greatest part of the building and complete it by the beginning of the new school year. The beginning of the novella describes, in a spirited and lively manner, the completion of the work, the genuine relationship of trust, the sincere discusions between teachers and pupils, the joyful anticipation of a better life in the new surroundings that they have created by themselves. Suddenly a state commission appears, finds everything to be "quite in order" after a more than superficial inspection of the old premises, and assigns the new building to another institution. The despairing efforts of the director, whom a well-meaning member of the party apparatus even wants to help, are naturally futile. To struggle against the bureaucratic arbitrariness of the Stalin era is fruitless, however legitimate the complaint.

That is all. A strikingly accurate refutation of the sectarian-bureaucratic legend that a genuine and active enthusiasm existed in the Stalin era. That there was indeed enthusiasm has not been disputed by any reasonable person. The legend begins with the idea that socialist enthusiasm of this kind could develop productively "alongside" and unhindered (indeed fostered) by the "personality cult". In Solzhenitsyn's work we see such a burst of enthusiasm together with the typical fate prepared for it by the Stalinist apparatus. As with Solzhenitsyn's other writings, this novella concludes just when the problem stands before us in all its plasticity without so much as a hint of the threads of human fate which lead to present-day man. The extensive framework too—again in the true manner of the novella—is drawn tightly: neither the description of the preceding sabotage on the part of the authorities nor the description of the final arbitrary action of the higher apparatus moves above a report of the bare, albeit convincing facts. Here too Solzhenitsyn, with his economical, objective, non-interpretative descriptive methods, succeeds in rendering conspicuous what is typical in these facts. Of course, this is not a merely technical question; this important design can only succeed because Solzhenitsyn is able to bring to life all his characters and their situations through his method of suggestive description. The genesis and the internal entanglements of the bureaucracy and the personal career-interests which are at work behind the "sublime" objectivity of the "cause" are beyond the story's scope; in the novella they appear only as an obvious but universal generality. The bureaucrats are presented to us—in their inhumanity which is cloaked in objectivity—in an extremely graphic manner, but neither socially nor humanly, are they illuminated from within. The initial enthusiasm of the teachers and pupils is described in more detail, again of course within this laconic novella style; so much so that the occasional reminders of the "Communist Saturdays" of the civil war era do not at all have the effect of clichés. However, the conclusion once again comes abruptly—though this of course is sanctioned by the form of the novella; the curtain falls after the unfolding of the bare facts; and what about the real, burning problems—how have these (and similar) experiences and events affected the teachers and pupils? How have they shaped their further lives? What kind of persons have they become in contemporary life? The questions are not answered. The conclusion is concretized only to the point of raising these questions in the minds of informed readers, questions which long reverberate and remain alive. Once again then—and this time in a far more concrete manner—there appears, much more strongly, an imperative reference to the central problems of today arising from the Stalinist past. Thus this novella cannot possess the inner completeness, roundness, and coherence of *One Day in the Life of Ivan Denisovich*, and for this reason it is not, in purely artistic terms, on the same level. However, as an exploration of the future this novella represents a great advance on his earlier works.

4.

No one can now predict when this advance will be completed and whether by Solzhenitsyn or by others. Solzhenitsyn is of course not the only one who is exploring these connections between yesterday and today. (It is perhaps sufficient to mention Nekrasov.) No one can predict how resolute efforts to unravel the present via an illumination of the Stalin era and thus of the human and moral antecedents of almost everyone active in public life today will turn out in reality. Crucial to this approach will be the course of social existence, of the self-renewal and reinforcement of socialist consciousness in the socialist countries, above all in the Soviet Union; however, every Marxist must take into consideration the necessarily uneven development of ideology, especially in literature and art.

Our description must thus stop at the statement of the inevitability of the "That" in this question, and leave the questions of "How" and "By Whom" completely open. This much is certain: there are powerful obstacles to and restraints upon this new development of socialist realism. Above all there is the resistance of those who have, or at least seem to have, remained faithful to Stalinist doctrines and methods. Their open opposition to any renewal has meanwhile been toned down by many events, it is true, but these people acquired a tactical adroitness in the Stalinist school. Under certain circumstances, indirectly invoked constraints could do more harm to the coming, often inwardly insecure new writers than could brutal administrative measures of the old style. (Of course there is no lack of such measures, and they too can do a great deal of harm.)

On the other hand, this movement toward the really new can be inhibited and misled, on the level of literary technique, by the provincial intellectual controversies concerning modernity that stand in the foreground today. We mentioned earlier that nothing of importance can be achieved in such ways, since artistically the point is to overcome the view of life which has given rise to the majority of literary trends based on naturalism. As long as many writers are fixated on such technical solutions, and given relatively elastic tactics on the part of the sectarian supporters of Stalin, the situation of the nineteen-thirties depicted here can very easily repeat itself. For instance, a Durrell-like "style" can be used to divert attention away from the real problems of the age. Naturally there are phenomena even in this area that must be taken seriously. The Stalinist era shook many people's faith in socialism. Considered subjectively the resulting doubts and disappointments may be completely honest and sincere and yet, when one endeavours to express them, could very easily lead to a mere slavish imitation of Western trends. And even when such works are interesting from a purely artistic stand-point, they are still largely unable to free themselves from a certain decadence. For the vision of Kafka, for example, is in-deed directed at the dark nihilism of the Hitler era, at some-thing fatal and real; the nothingness of a Beckett, however, is a mere game with fictitious abysses that no longer correspond to anything of importance in historical reality. I am well aware that for over a century intellectual circles have held scepticism and pessimism in much higher esteem than the belief in a great cause of human development, whose manifestations may well have been problematic in the short term. However, Goethe's words at Valmy are more truly prophetic than the statement that women will become hyenas; and in Goethe's works these words foreshadow the last Faust monologue. Shelley is more original and enduring than Chateaubriand, and Keller learnt more, and more fruitfully, from 1848 than did Stifter. And in the same way, all future development in world history and world literature depends above all on those whom the Stalin era has spurred on to deepen their socialist convictions and give them contemporary relevance. Even the most honest and most gifted of those who have lost their convictions and produce "interesting works" in the wake of Western trends will be made to appear as mere imitators by the emergence of the yet dormant forces which will determine the future.

To repeat, it is not my intention to raise the problem of avant-gardism here. I am aware that writers like Brecht, Thomas Wolfe, in his later works, Elsa Morant, Heinrich Böll and others have created important, original and presumably lasting works. The point here is only that a disillusionment with socialism, combined with the stylistic forms of Western alienated scepticism, can only produce a second-rate imitative work. It is perhaps superfluous to say that honest people can only conquer their disillusionment in life itself, in their own lives, in a confrontation with socio-historical reality. Literary argument is of no avail, and administrative measures will succeed even better than aristocratic esotericism had done in strengthening mere fashion, while honest seekers will be repelled from socialism more violently than ever before. Such formal experiments are wholly alien to Solzhenitsyn and writers like him. They are attempting to work, humanly and intellectually, socially and artistically, toward the reality which has always been the starting point of genuinely new forms in art. This can be seen in Solzhenitsyn's work to date.

The connections between it and the problems of contemporary renewal of Marxism are also easily identifiable. Any further anticipatory judgement concerning the style of the coming period would be theoretically an empty scholasticism, artistically a *Beckmesserei*.* What has become apparent so far is the following: any future great literature of a revitalized socialism cannot possibly, least of all where the all-important questions of form are concerned, be a straightforward continuation of the first upsurge of the nineteen-twenties, nor a return to it. The structure of the conflicts, the qualitative character of human beings and their relations with each other have undergone a fundamental change since that time. And every genuine style originates when writers discern in contemporary life those specific dynamic and structural forms most deeply characteristic of it, and when they are able—and here we see true originality—to discover a mirror in which the deepest and most typical essence of those forms is most appropriately reflected. The writers of the nineteen-twenties portrayed the turbulent transition from bourgeois to socialist society. At that time the path led from the security of the age of peace—which of course was objectively undermined—via war and civil war to socialism. Ostensibly, people were faced with the dramatic necessity of choosing the side to which they wished to belong; frequently—and often very dramatically—they had to move from one class into another. These and similar facts of life determined the style of socialist realism in the nineteen-twenties. The structure and dynamics of present-day dilemmas are very different. External dramatic conflicts are rare exceptions. The surface of social life often appears to change little over long periods of time, and even the visible changes develop slowly and gradually. By contrast, for decades a radical transformation has been taking place in the inner lives of human beings, a transformation which is already affecting the surface of society and which

* The reference is to a captious character in the *Meistersinger—Trans.*

will attain a growing significance in shaping the external forms of life. However, in the past and in the present the accent falls on the inner, ethical life of man, on the ethical decisions which he perhaps cannot express outwardly. But it would be wrong to see in this artistic predominance of inwardness an analogy to certain Western trends where the apparently absolute dominance of alienation produced an ostensibly boundless but in reality impotent inner life. What is meant here is a chain of internal decisions, and for the time being the majority of these can only rarely be released in visible actions. The distinguishing characteristic of this chain, however, is a drama that is often heightened into tragedy. It depends on how quickly and deeply these people recognize the danger of the Stalinist period, how they react toward it and how their collected experiences, their moral victory or failure, their steadfastness, their collapse or conformism and their capitulation influence their present actions. And it is plain that the most genuine moral victory is gained by strengthening and deepening real Marxist and socialist convictions through the rejection of Stalinist distortions, while remaining receptive to new problems.

There is no need to go further since it is not my intention here to describe, even in outline, the whole of the present, its historical genesis and the typical variations of human modes of behaviour. My intention was to show the conditions of life which demand that socialist realism should develop a different style than the one dictated by the reality of the nineteen-twenties for the literature of that time, and it appears to me that even these few intimations go some way towards this goal. And this statement must suffice. I can only add that this is the soil on which Solzhenitsyn's novella form grew. Where future writers will seek their points of contact is their own affair. "Je prends mon bien où je le trouve" was always the motto of original and significant writers; they run the risk implicit in every choice, namely whether the "mon bien" is a genuine possession and whether it is always entered upon with pleasure and a sense of responsibility; in the case of the lesser lights this gamble may be taken thoughtlessly frivolously. However successful theory might be in describing in advance the general social preconditions of such a transformation (of life into art), it must needs confine itself to this and speak *post festum* about any concrete artistic production.

(1964)

11. *Solzhenitsyn's novels*

IN THE previous essay I argued the case that Solzhenitsyn's novellas represent a significant step in the renewal of the great traditions of the socialist realism of the nineteen-twenties. The question of whether he himself would bring about the re-birth of socialist realism and its new growth into a significant world literature was one that I cautiously left open. I can now state with pleasure that I was far too cautious: Solzhenitsyn's two new novels represent a new high point in contemporary world literature.

Only in the concluding remarks can I enter into the ideological and aesthetical limitations of these works.

My prediction that this new upsurge could not be simply a straightforward and immediate continuation of the past golden age was borne out to an even greater extent. The very fact that, then as now, the really outstanding writers concern themselves with the central social and human questions of their age, both directly and in their innermost intentions, necessitates a qualitative difference in content and form. The highly dramatic destruction of the antagonistic class structure inherited from Czarism has very little in common—externally and internally, in content and in form—with the overcoming of the Stalinist period that has obviously now become unavoidable. The same is true of artistic expression. Of course historical continuity in the most general sense is nevertheless irrevocable, but it operates in an irregular way. With the first imperialist war, with the answering of the questions it raised by the great October Days of 1917, a new global condition became reality. No poet or thinker who

33

wishes to comprehend and express this faithfully can ignore completely the general uniformity of this new global condition. The more honestly he endeavours to represent the specific aspects of his present and the more intensively he wishes to meet the "challenges of the day", the less can he ignore it. However, the continuity of the problems thus arising, if it is really carried through, must often, indeed most of the time, appear as an abrupt discontinuity of the individual stages.

So it was and so it is in social reality itself. Already in 1921, Lenin's introduction of the "New Economic Policy" was a sharp break with "War Communism", and not an unbroken, straightforward continuation of the latter with at best formal improvements. Such a discontinuity demonstrates above all the law of socially productive action. To be sure, there are frequently principles of rigid continuity even in powerful systems. But one can observe without difficulty that objectively and in the long run, the ensuing over-nervous attempts to avoid any crisis only contribute to the intensification of the crisis situation.

This statement is of particular importance to literature. For one cannot emphasize forcibly enough that genuine literature does not exist to prepare or propagate concrete formulae for current day-to-day *praxis*; nor of course to make the immediately private and personal, particular expressions of life, with no real existence, and which are ostensibly independent of the great social questions, into the sole subject of art. Great literature of all ages, from Homer to the present day, has, in the final analysis, "contented itself" with showing how a given social condition, a stage of development, a developmental tendency, has intrinsically influenced the course of human existence, human development, the dehumanization and alienation of man from himself. Since artistically this is inconceivable without a portrayal of the concrete social forces at work, there results a picture of social existence, based on this point of view, which is more lucid than that which social existence itself is able to invoke directly. For this reason, not unimportant effects can, under certain circumstances, originate in the social *praxis* of human beings though this is often not apparent on the surface. The bias of true art is distinguishable from the tendencies of ephemeral literature by the fact that in meeting the challenge of its time, the former is able to concentrate on the whole complex, on the true essence of social phenomena and not be obliged to provide specific solutions to mere day-to-day problems. Such solutions are implicit in social reality, in photographic illustrations, and they are of course, discoverable through *praxis*.

In this respect Solzhenitsyn is heir not only to the best tendencies in early socialist realism, but also to the great literary tradition, above all that of Tolstoy and Dostoevsky.

I.

Questions of style are always directly concerned with the specific expression of the present. Here we encounter what has hitherto been a completely obscure phenomena. One preliminary observation is necessary. The concepts of style employed in the history of art and literature have frequently hardened into *a priori* fetishes. Since we cannot enter into this question here, let us remark that in what follows we will speak of methods of composition which, although affected by content, are indeed formal, and which originate in the specific problem complex of a given stage of development. Despite a certain and artistically significant formal uniformity, these methods thus make possible—and in the case of the great artists actually inspire—extensive differentiations in content and, consequently, in form. It must be added that such specific creative methods of elucidating new and important complexes of social content by no means need establish their absolute dominance, not even for a specific stage. They may be important and influential innovations without even temporarily assuming a dominant monopolistic position in the production of their age (or even of their authors).

In order to classify the principle underlying the new formal features of Solzhenitsyn's novels, we must above all refer to Thomas Mann's *The Magic Mountain*. To see what is new in this novel we need merely recall that in its initial stages the great novel of realism was oriented towards the "totality" of objects found in the older ethics, in order to be able to portray the reality of society in its entirety, and at the same time in its sensuous and palpable unity. Even where the subject matter imposed extreme economy—Defoe's *Robinson Crusoe* comes to mind—this foundation of a totality of objects is plainly evident. When later the naturalism of the nineteenth century reduced the society it depicted to a "sociologically" determined "milieu" and its portrayal of character to what was occasionally and typically called the average, the abstract requirement of totality was retained with regard to both groups of objective reality, but henceforth only in the sense of a pseudo-scientific, "sociological" abstractness—which meant that the most important narrative and descriptive consistency of the "totality of objects", namely the totality of human reactions to them, was lost or at least receded sharply. It would be frivolous to claim that the old-style realism could be replaced by such a descriptive method, however inexorable its emergence; this would have meant the end of every historically relevant narrative method. The fact is, however, that the changes in the structure and dynamics of society created problems whose adequate reflection seemed to demand new methods of composition. These new developments frequently appeared during the crises of the world war and the socialist revolution. Although literary public opinion does not usually regard *The Magic Mountain* as an attempt at formal innovation, I believe that in this novel Thomas Mann was a more important innovator than were many of his contemporaries with their loud programmatical pronouncements (e.g. the "new objectivity"), above all because, as we shall see, he placed the problem of the totality of reactions at the centre of the composition.

The compositional innovation in *The Magic Mountain* may be described for the time being in a purely formal way, namely that the uniformity of the setting is made the immediate foundation of the narrative. The characters of this novel are removed from the "natural" location of their lives and movements, and are transplanted into new and artificial surroundings (here the sanatorium for consumptives). The major consequence of this is that the characters do not come into contact with each other, as so often in life and even more frequently in art, in "normal ways", i.e. they are not limited by birth, occupation, etc.; rather this "chance" common terrain of their present existence creates new fundamental forms of their human, intellectual and moral relations with each other. That there is here a certain kinship to certain form of the modern novella is revealed in the fact that the first draft of *The Magic Mountain* was a novella, an ironic parallel to *Death in Venice*, where the change of atmosphere following the transposition into completely new surroundings was the actual cause that led the hero's hitherto latent ideological conflict into a tragicomical explosion. The growth of the novella into a universal novel of this style (we will be able to discern a similar transition in Solzhenitsyn's works) only points to the presence of similar factors in their geneses and to an extremely general definition of their relationship to reality, but hardly signifies a decisive inner material connection. The immediate motif of this development in the case of Thomas Mann is his concern to endow his characters' reactions to their new environment with a universal breadth and depth. The new surroundings bring about the formal change of function: in the final analysis Venice as a location is only incidental to the final eruption of the constant latent conflict in the life of Gustav von Aschenbach. By contrast, although the sanatorium for consumptives is on the one hand a mere setting, on the other hand, in accordance with its nature, it arouses in the characters—precisely because it is a more or less forced common place of residence of characters who for the most part first come into contact with each other here—the desire to become aware of and come to terms with the problems of life of which they had never been made aware at home. The sanatorium is thus the factual, immediate trigger of ideological problems which were everywhere latent but which only here emerge into consciousness with all their contradictions.

It is of no importance here to know to what extent Thomas Mann himself was aware of this connection when he accomplished the transition from the novella to this special and new kind of mode. It is certain that similar modes of composition appeared increasingly, if not systematically, after 1917, when ideological problems acquired immediate social significance and came into the forefront of human life more than ever before.

An instance is the almost simultaneous publication with *The Magic Mountain*, of Sinclair Lewis' *Martin Arrowsmith*. The latter, to be sure, is at the same time a background to an *Erziehungsroman**, certain elements of which are also present in Thomas Mann's work. A further example, though a fragmentary one, is Musil's *The Man Without Qualities* in which the planned "great action", which is supposed to conceal the disintegration of the Habsburg Monarchy and for this very reason compels awareness of it, plays the same role as the sanatorium. It is evident that a new setting is not the only social phenomenon to stimulate new analysis, but that any socially objective reality in which such an unaccustomed, reaction-provoking force is inherent, will have this effect. The new significance attached to heterogeneous, not immedi-

* biographical novel dealing with the development of a character—*Trans.*

ately related utterances, is the decisive formal factor. The inner discontinuity of the work is formally due to the fact that Musil puts aside his original design (and thus its artistically necessary descriptive method) and turns to the portrayal of quite different problems. This composition also appears in the immediate present, as the vehicle for versatile satire, in Böll's *Absent Without Leave*. Here a "sensational" local trial in a small German town produce a series of reactions which, although—or rather because—they are so muted stamp the whole as provincial.

As a final example let us recall the intellectually very eminent work from the period of flowering of socialist realism, Makarenko's *The Road to Life: an epic of education*. Here this compositional motif appears, with rare clarity, as the educational workshop of Makarenko the teacher. In it youths who have become vagabonds, indeed frequently criminals, are to be re-educated as new socialist human beings; thus ideological reactions, usually in the form of cathartic acts of crisis, play a central role as an effective force in the process of the characters' self-discovery (or self-loss). The uniqueness of this form is naturally extremely closely connected with its socialist content.

Considered in terms of scholarly aesthetics or literary history, these works exhibit little evidence of a formal congruity; as far as their so-called "influence" on each other is concerned, it is extremely probable that no connections whatever exist between them. Nevertheless, or so I believe, this mode of composition has originated everywhere in similar, genuinely socio-aesthetic requirements. From a wider perspective, neither naturalism nor this, its genuine artistic overcoming, should be seen as simply accidental or purely individually determined. For the development of capitalism, owing to its universality, owing to its consequent common style of life, frequently forced into the background those forms of the representative type of the—at least inwardly—

significant personalities whose fates initially determined the novel's form; it also largely made into the dominant consideration the prejudice that the external common life style whose only permissible variant was the pathological, was the true expression of a socially valid universality. The realization that these prejudices are intellectually and artistically untenable involves various innovations in the art of the novel.

Any attempt to illuminate the social and intellectual foundations of these innovations leads us to a revaluation of the ways in which reality is to be mastered; and this revaluation encompasses every aspect of our attempts to understand reality. The fact that this new relationship appeared in a distinct form first of all in the natural sciences does not detract from its universality and its—of course fundamentally different—applicability to literature, but on the contrary imparts to the latter a universality which exceeds by far the merely formal. We mean the method of cognition which, proceeding from the natural sciences, has become widespread in the social sciences, namely the replacement of the mere theoretical combination of causal series of causal connections by the method of statistical probability. Of course it is not possible to treat the connections and contrasts between the two methods in any detail at this point (or to discuss the early prejudices which chose to regard the new principle as incompatible with causality). My sole concern here is to establish that individual causal series, whose starting points (and, especially in social terms, end points) are identical, can be grouped together for the purpose of analysing how the individual elements (in social terms: human beings) react in practice to the causal impetus here at work. For the natural sciences, this depended above all on how the relationship between normal and divergent reactions was expressed mathematically. In the process it becomes apparent that there is a form of inherent order as valid as the forms it has superseded. In addition, it has two further advantages. On the one hand these forms can now be expressed in a more sophisticated fashion; on the other hand it reveals the nature of the separate factors that constitute the inherent order, though for the most part it does so in a negative way, by registering deviations from the dominant order.

Of course, since the purpose of this method is to eliminate anthropomorphic elements and to treat everything homogeneously in purely numerical terms, it can by no means serve directly as a model for artistic portrayals or social reality, not even in their sociological variants, or what in the exact sciences serves as the foundation of any understanding of reality, namely the use of the particular as the abstract, complementary, polar antithesis of the universal, can be expressed directly, in non-anthropomorphic and mathematical abstractions, as statistical probability. If it is true, as everywhere in society, that the individuality of each member of society consists in mere separateness, then the patterns of his behaviour can here again be expressed in terms of mathematical probability, although even here the deviations, if they are to be correctly evaluated, often demand a degree of concreteness exceeding the merely statistical. An attempt at a more or less direct transposition—e.g. the inclusion of photographs of reality already comprehended scientifically in narrative works, as was often done in the "new objectivity"—can thus only lead to an inferior revival of sociological naturalism.

For the elementary social fact that mere separateness, as an element of objective events, has given rise to the individual human being, to individuality (viewed, in the first instance, not in terms of value, but as a mere fact) can no doubt be "put into parentheses" by the non-anthropomorphic social sciences and thus be comprehended with statistical exactness. However, when we come to literature, where there can be no question of excluding the anthropomorphic, the general laws, founded on the totality and dynamics of man and society, can no longer be eliminated. A real literary adaptation of the universal quality and global view which attain their scientific form in statistical probability must thus—without losing its basis in social reality—obtain a qualitatively different form, a transformation into something pre-eminently qualitative. This is, ultimately, an identical mode of being, but it gives rise to an essentially different mimetic understanding in literature. In the last analysis the order arrived at by organizing individuals with social and personal dimensions according to their typical reactions to an important question posed by their lives, has only a formal congruity with the ordering of particular and general found in the patterns of statistical probability. Statistical probability must thus appear as the direct antithesis of literary understanding in all individual questions of the creative reproduction of existence, inasmuch as artistic totalities select for emphasis qualitatively typical examples from what is a mere aggregate represented in terms of statistical laws and contrast them with those types which, in mathematical-statistical totalities, largely figure as mere deviations from the predominant trend. This is the fundamental existential pattern of the totality of reactions. However, the ultimate similarity of the fundamental principal is maintained throughout this process of restructuring: the conscious creation of a concrete setting is not intended primarily as a mere theatre for individual-typical events in relation to which it would otherwise necessarily preserve a certain element of chance. It is intended instead as a kind of social phenomena whose "That" and "How" ask of human beings the questions crucial to them at the moment, or which by its existence, by the existence of human beings within it, forces these questions into their consciousness and compels answers to them. Thus this new mode of narrative composition arises.

Above all, there is now no further need for a unified plot (the extremes, above all Thomas Mann and Makarenko come to mind). This already occurs in the earlier and also more recent naturalist pictures of society. Now in the latter case the absence of a unified plot must necessarily result in a static description of the characters and a reduction of their human existence to mere particularity, which to be sure usually aims at the average. In the new type of novel which we have been investigating, the very absence of a unified plot results in a highly dynamic narrative and in an internal drama. For the social existence symbolized in the uniform setting, whose nature is adjusted to the characters, is not merely a milieu to which the characters simply submit and by which they are condemned to passivity. This social existence is rather the social force (or possibly only the social cause) which, when the characters come into contact with it, urges them to achieve an awareness of and to master the crucial ideological and practical problems of their relationship to their own social existence. This generates a whole series of individual scenes in which—both individually and in their interrelation—a high and concentrated drama can be inherent. They need by no means be combined into a unified plot, and indeed rarely are. However, since the socially uniform setting encourages, indeed provokes individual decisions, since they are continuously at work in a social sense, and although (or precisely because) the reactions triggered reveal the greatest dissimilarities, even antitheses, dramatically moving, uniformly narrative connections can originate in individual scenes which appear to be unrelated; these connections can then be combined by narrative means into a totality of human reactions to an important problem complex.

The only formal requirement here is that the surroundings (or an occurrence) should not be natural and self-evident to the characters and that they be capable of bringing about an effect which triggers a characteristic reaction. Naturally such reactions can originate at any time and in any place. Although a character's "natural" surroundings, e.g. the family, may also have a similar effect on him, they can often remain a completely indifferent setting which induces no reaction of any importance in him; this can apply even to those whose lives are extremely closely bound to these "natural" surroundings. Even in the case of surroundings which actually comprise extremely heterogeneous human types (school, office, etc.), an effect so arranged is by no means inevitable. Sinclair Lewis must directly stylize his selection of figures and their formation in such a way as to effect a self-revelation of the kind intended here; in Böll by contrast the legal proceedings, which for the provincial town are eccentric and exciting, create "automatically" such an atmosphere of a self- and other-revealing totality of reactions. This only shows, however, how little one can generalize mechanically and formally about that which we have required of form. Certainly it is by no means universally necessary that all characters feel themselves called upon to give an answer at all to the questions put to them by their social existence. Here it depends above all on whether this socially necessary reality—which however influences the individual characters from without— is simply accepted as a "normal" existence, as a "natural" continuation of their previous lives, or whether such a contact of a character's own life with a sphere of social reality will cause him to regard his existence and its meaning for himself and for his fellow man with new eyes, and to make himself and others aware of it. At this level of questioning then, it is still irrelevant whether the answers arising therefore turn out to be positive or negative.

From the standpoint of art it is obvious that on the average these spontaneously released reactions will be less significant in proportion as such "settings" represent the result of a social necessity valid for all the characters concerned or of a radical (possibly only a temporary) change in their everyday lives. The boundaries, as in the case of all social phenomena, are of course fluid. Sinclair Lewis must occasionally employ artificial methods in order to throw into bold relief his characters' reactions to the combination of medicine and science as a profession; thus a large number of his characters behave in an indifferent or passive manner. But one must not forget that in *The Magic Mountain* too, where a departure from normal everyday life is the basis of the novel, the confrontation with sickness, with the perspectives and reality of their own deaths tears only a fraction of those exiled to the sanatorium away from their external, accustomed way of life. Many will simply inwardly avoid such confrontations and, despite their changed conditions, endeavour to continue their old way of life unchanged and without taking stock of themselves anew. Of course, we find here an important difference of emphasis: in Sinclair Lewis such characters, when their general adaptation is not compressed and concretized into an answer, become simple products of their milieu whose behaviour lies quite outside the dialectic of the novel, while in *The Magic Mountain* this is raised to a factor which helps to determine the whole. One might say that it involves a qualitative inversion of statistical probability: the majority of the indifferent, unchanging attitudes correspond —with some chance of error—to the general, scientifically attainable probability of reactions, whereas the more passionate viewpoints thrust into the foreground usually come under the heading of deviations from the "normal". Disregarding all these reservations, however, it can be said that this artistic portrayal is aimed precisely at representing a social problem complex in such a way that it triggers very specific alternative decisions on the part of the characters who come into contact with it. The less artificial this activating factor appears, the greater are the prospects of a new, dynamic formulation of an ideologically active relationship between the individual characters and the society in which they must live and operate.

The way in which this dynamic originates and operates has very far-reaching aesthetic consequences for the perfection of this new form. It is a necesary and direct consequence of the subject we have been pursuing that the interrelations depicted usually have a unique explosiveness. At the same time it does not follow from the intrinsic character of such reflections on the inner relation of individual characters to the actual problem complexes of society that a temporal-causal continuity, a step-by-step sequence which constitutes the essence of the plot—*must* necessarily exist. Measured against the standard of the classical novel, such works consist of a series of often seemingly unconnected episodes concentrated in the manner of the novella. However, the less of a connection in the old narrative sense exists between them, the more pronounced are their ideological cross-references, whether they be of a mutually supporting or of a destructively contradicting kind. If these are carried to their logical conclusion, there arises a largely new form of narrative synthesis which at this point demonstrates the kinship between its theoretical roots and its conception of a reality corresponding to statistical laws. That is to say all these individual reactions, which in the novella often appear to be autonomous, now constitute a uniform dynamic totality, since every such individually represented reaction refers intellectually to all the others, inasmuch as both confirmation and contradiction appear socially as aspects of a unified process. This process, with its rich and varied dynamic, here constitutes the principle of unity—that which in earlier works of fiction was called upon to express the unity of the plot and the totality of objects. Thus while this kind of portrayal ostensibly departed from the older creative methods even further than it had from the milieu pictures of naturalism, it in fact achieved the contrary (if we set aside mere descriptive statistics and the particularism of the average)—namely the renewal of its deepest essence: the dynamic conception of the totality of society with the individual character as its fundamental fact, as its immediate motor force, as the direct (if not always adequate) expression of the motive trends which deeply characterize this whole. In other words, it is a question of a totality of reactions.

2.

In earlier literature, this mode of expression, initiated by
Thomas Mann, attained its purest form in Makarenko's work.
In it the realization of the possibility of a completely new
way of life, through a concentration of passionate and
dramatic, personal and social controversies between a new
social form and the old one, thrusts all the motive factors
mentioned here onto the highest extensive and, above all,
intensive level. The reason for this lies in the subject matter.
The socially invoked confrontation of man with himself in
the sanatorium is a mere possibility—one which, to be sure,
is closely connected with the fact that he has been displaced
there—to which the characters may well react by rejecting
any questions of this kind. In Makarenko, by contrast, the
educational institution for delinquent children representing
an attempt to transform them into socialists—is determined
socially and teleologically from the very outset. When an
individual refuses to respond to the new social surroundings
or ignores the questions raised by them, his act contains in
itself an element of negation, and even as a negation constitutes
a certain reaction. In the world of *The Magic Mountain*,
which necessitates no action, action must be expressed as a
choice, a decision, a reaction within the action. In Makarenko's
work, the new settings universalize the reactions to them;
such a general activity on the part of the surroundings amounts
to a questioning of society itself, in contrast to a mere release
of society's potentialities, and determines the special character
of Makarenko's world. This difference, which as the dynamic
motor of the movement decisively influences the narrative
composition, becomes an immediate factor in its aesthetic
character. But one must never forget that this aesthetic
dynamic has its real roots and hence too its adequate mimesis
in the nature of social existence itself.

For this reason it is no coincidence that this manner of

portraying an existence which does more than present the occasion for such answers, and which universally and directly sets them in motion, is a way of portraying existence under socialism in contrast to capitalism. This is only true if it is seen and portrayed in the true spirit of Marx, in accordance with the great doctrine that man makes his own history, which if applied to such complexes, is concretized as "the educator must himself be educated". This is the antithesis which excludes both the bourgeois and the merely Utopian attitudes. For in Makarenko the producing of alternative decisions is not merely intended to educate the youths who have gone astray to be true human beings, indeed socialist human beings, but also to make the conscious creator of such cathartic and salutary crises, namely the educator himself, into a conscious teacher of socialist life for socialists. In contrast to this, when, as in Thomas Mann, the characters are only confronted spontaneously with their existence, when the only goal set is their physical recovery, then the agents of this recovery, i.e. the doctors, are only spectators of, but not necessarily actors in the ideological drama, which they themselves bring about. The educator in Makarenko's work, by contrast, is a centrally active main figure in all the cathartic scenes which constitute the substance of this novel.

It is thus no accident that Solzhenitsyn's novels, which constitute an important contemporary variant of the new novel latch on to this formal trend at this point. It goes without saying that "latch on" is here intended in a purely objective historical sense. Whether Solzhenitsyn ever read Makarenko's novel and if so, with what impression, cannot be answered by this writer; in any case it is not decisive. In Makarenko, there is objectively an original advance on Thomas Mann's innovation, irrespective of whether Makarenko ever read Thomas Mann's novel. The progress of sociohistorical existence has created and developed this descriptive method quite independently of any so-called "influences".

Makarenko is a great story-teller of the age of the heroic rise of socialism, Solzhenitsyn a significant portrayer of its greatest crisis until now. This is the origin of the difference, indeed the contrast between their concrete lines of artistic inquiry. The further development of the descriptive method treated here, which is completed by Solzhenitsyn, originates primarily in an historical situation. The extension, the "totalization" of the earlier famous novella represents with organic necessity not only an increase in the number of internees from a small group ultimately centred around one individual into a considerable part of the population of the entire country; it also requires that the initiators—the executors in organization and practice of this internment of huge masses of human beings which lasted for decades—be likewise described more extensively and concretely, indeed that their sheer numbers, represented through individuals, must produce an artistic contrast to their victims. Only then do the "settings" that ask questions of the characters acquire a concrete, socially-determined universality and dynamic. In the final analysis, the social fact remains that the internment camp puts irresistibly and spontaneously its provocative, vital questions to its victims and to its organizers, and forces everyone concerned to reconcile the way of life that henceforth he can and must lead with the objective possibilities of his situation and at the same time with those of his human nature.

Solzhenitsyn's method of composition is to take the two groups, whose lives are irrevocably bound up with each other, but whose ends and means are completely opposed and to intensify the inner drama between them to the greatest possible extent through an interplay of questions and answers. For this reason the place of internment is no longer an average one as it was in *One Day in the Life of Ivan D.* The author underlines this by the fact that the one day depicted is relatively pleasant and not concentrated into tragedy; it is precisely the "first circle" of Hell, the workshop of what are in this context privileged specialists who work in extreme secrecy preparing inventions considered by the system as important to its *praxis*. When he is taken away, the internee, Nerzhin, of whom we shall have more to say later, says: "Where we're going—that's Hell. [Where we have been] is the best, the highest, the first circle of hell. It's almost paradise . . ."[1] No detailed commentary is needed to show that the stasis of the earlier novella, although it was so immediately explosive, is thus dynamically intensified at its very foundations: here every internee is confronted not only by the slender hope of liberation, but by a very real threat of a more infernal region of hell. His behaviour is thus permanently put on trial in a twofold and dynamic maner. Not only does it contain struggles for sheer self-preservation, as in the novella, but under the constant threat of falling even further into the abyss there arrive new questions, each of which can, and often really does, trigger off resistance.

This extension, differentiation, this hierarchical process refers, however, to the active class among the characters, to the executive organization of these camps—again in contrast to the novella in which only the immediate supervisory organs of the penal system figure. This too helps to heighten the dynamic of the novel. For when the agents of authority come on the scene entering into contact both with the prisoners and their own organization, then not only does each of their actions affect the objects of their activities, but everything that each character in the apparatus does or fails to do has repercussions on his own immediate existence. Thus on this side too there arises a dramatization shaded into individual details. Through their activities the representatives of authority construct their own lives, both outwardly with regard to the advancement or destruction of their careers, and inwardly

[1] Alexander Solzhenitsyn, *The First Circle* (London, Fontana, 1970, translated by Michael Guybon) p. 699.

in the sense of self-preservation or self-alienation. These reactions, which are always described as individual answers to the momentary concrete requirements of the apparatus, thus differentiate this group of characters as well, again both from without and from within, both as behavioural requirements made of every character in consequence of his position on the bureaucratic ladder, and everywhere in consequence of individual personal reactions to these requirements.

This dynamic question-and-answer structure is not confined to the immediate agents of the camp administration. The Stalinist system has a high degree of coherence and universality. Probably not one character could say from the outset with complete assurance that his own life would remain unaffected by dilemmas. Everyday life can at any moment create situations of a passive or active nature which compel such decisions. Since the author is concerned here with the choices exercised by individuals, the reproduction of movements within and arising out of the society as a whole is well calculated both to intensify and to compress the dynamics of the individual choices.

The connection originates in the monolithic character of the apparatus. Here Solzhenitsyn refers back to its ultimate principles by showing how the hierarchy reaches all the way from the characters who are, as it were, fortuitously and sometimes quite passively implicated in it, up to Stalin himself. As in Walter Scott's classical historical novels, the central figure appears only episodically: Stalin is seen only on a single occasion. Because of this, the presence of the man who, in theory and in practice is the central figure of this world plays a twofold compositional role which Solzhenitsyn exploits with great artistry. First, Stalin appears as the boss of the entire apparatus; upon his opinion, indeed upon his mere impressions of a report for example depends the fate of even his highest placed underling. In this case a fairly important "boss" is commanded to present a report on the deadline by which a new listening-in device is to be ready for use. The high-ranking employee, Abakumov, knows that the deadline cannot be met; nevertheless he both slants his report to Stalin and arranges matters in the "first circle" of hell so that when the fatal question comes it can be answered positively. The period of waiting for the audience, like the audience itself, is filled with tension concerning the tone in which Stalin will ask and how he will receive Abukumov's answers. This tension rises during the stages of preparation and in the conversation itself, until it is released when the overworked Stalin finally forgets to raise the problem for discussion and Abakumov can—for the time being—go home reassured.

Secondly, Stalin himself is presented to us in a tired, over-worked mood which is also expressed in lonely inner monologues. Solzhenitsyn again proves himself a penetrating, significant artist by never dwelling on petty psychological considerations, whether of an accusing or excusing character. Instead he concentrates the situation of the inner monologue directly on the central questions, both political and human, of Stalin's historical existence. Thus, in the context of a problem of education he makes him reflect on his relationship with Lenin: "This has all been Lenin's fault, though it is still too early to say so aloud. 'Any cook should be able to run the country.' . . . What had Lenin actually meant by this? Did he mean they should take a day off every week to work in the local Soviet. A cook is a cook and his job is to get the dinner ready, whereas telling other people what to do is a highly skilled business; it can only be done by specially selected and trained personnel who have been toughened by years of experience, while in turn the control of this personnel could only be entrusted to one pair of hands—the practised hands of the leader."[2] Stalin here formulates the deeply anti-democratic spirit of his methods of leadership with a degree of precision that would be difficult to improve upon. For

[2] Ibid, p. 121.

socialism—and Lenin never lost sight of this fact—is far less concerned with the formal aspects of democracy (universal suffrage, secret ballot, etc.) than with the actual democratization of the whole of everyday human life. Lenin's cook is then above all a perspective, a goal, the transmission of an ancient democratic heritage to its final social fulfilment, which is only possible under socialism. Thus in his reflections on Tolstoy's attitude toward culture, the present author wrote some decades ago: "In this connection, the peasant, who according to Tolstoy possesses the criteria of art and correctly judges art, appears *as a link in the historical chain that leads from Molière's maid to Lenin's cook who administers the state.*"[3]

The Stalinist principle of bureaucratization to the most minute degree thus determines for better or worse the fate of all who work in the centralized apparatus. The atmosphere of the reception in Stalin's office oscillating between fear and hope is only a concentrated model of all intercourse within such an apparatus. This is not only a matter of the underling's constant adaption to the momentary will of his superior. The situation can also be reversed, when the former believes himself to be in possession of the means of bringing down the latter. The relentless adaptation by all to the fear and hope exuded in concentrated form by Stalin's antechamber and reception rooms is in this way really the model by which the executive organs of the internment camp allow their behaviour and their attitude toward their own lives to be guided. And naturally, this applies above all to them, but not to them alone. For the all-inclusive extension of the system enables it to take its objects from all spheres of life; this of course results in a very large number of people being thrust into a situation where they must take decisions which fall within the immediate scope of the great apparatus. In such cases, the apparatus' method operates objectively, but its

[3] Georg Lukács, *Tolstoi und die Probleme des Realismus, werke Vol. 5, Probleme des Realismus II* (Luchterhand, Neuwied and Berlin, 1964) p. 258

universality, influence, etc. necessarily cause its logic and the aberrations which it creates to have also a subjective influence on such a decision.

Solzhenitsyn understands such cases also. The young diplomat, Councillor Innokenty Volodin, who is about to receive the distinction of a transfer to Paris, learns by chance that a doctor, Professor Dobroumov, whom he has admired for many years, is said to have committed an indiscretion which, in Volodin's view, is not in itself wrong. Now his freedom, his existence are threatened. Should he warn him, exhort him to caution? In nervous haste Volodin considers whether his identity could be established by a telephone call from a public box and the like, until the thought strikes him: "If you always look over your shoulder, how can you still remain a human being?"[4] And he does call Dobroumov. Because of the excessive caution of the latter's wife the warning is unsuccessful. But Volodin appears again and again in the course of this extensive novel plagued by fear and hope until at the end he is in fact arrested, and we witness the de-humanizing degradation that even the formal admission to such prisons necessarily involves. The social aspect of camp administration naturally reappears frequently, even in the shape of more or less conforming intellectuals, and shows how great a part of the characters' everyday life is subject to this manipulation.

Above all the class of those wielding immediate power is important. Again Solzhenitsyn demonstrates his great talent for concise characterization, for observing or inventing situations which compel the characters to reveal—not passively but in response to those situations—their practical relations to society, to their own concrete activity within it and thus to themselves. Throughout the whole concrete range of external and internal variants, the social and human laws of such a way of life come to light vividly and extremely unambiguously.

[4] *The First Circle*, p. 14

Not for nothing did Spinoza and, following him, Goethe point out the "two greatest enemies of man," namely the emotions of fear and hope. Institutions whose functioning rests on the daily mobilization of precisely these emotions must necessarily "educate" the people yoked to it and devotedly serving it to inner passivity and thus to the loss of their humanity. This occurs, more or less, in most bureaucracies which are sufficiently influential to subordinate completely, even inwardly, those in thrall to them. Should bureaucracy become the dominant mode of life of those participating in it, should the decisions dictated by it determine their way of life entirely, then inevitably the tactics of the apparatus, dictated by its day-to-day needs, become the ultimate judge of all decisions between good and evil. And since no truly objective social norms of action can arise from this situation, every participating individual is thrown back into a purely particular subjectivity and is fatally ruled by fear and hope, by means of which the truly social activity of man degenerates into an often inhuman passivity in which officiousness takes the place of genuine action.

Here the inner dynamic of this society is revealed in a repeated ebb and flow. Its basic form rests on the fact that such people, in their external lives, in their particular existence, appear to represent the extreme of permanent activity, but at the same time—and indeed in the same acts in which this activity directly and visibly culminates—their inner nature remains completely passive and, in the sense of a genuine humanity they remain uniformly shallow. Every step they take is determined neither by objective necessities, namely by actual social requirements of the moment, nor by the necessities of their own individual paths, i.e. the real individual ego of people realizing themselves in social *praxis*. Instead they are motivated by purely tactical considerations concerning the momentary situation—e.g. as to which decisions from higher places is to be regarded as correct, as promoting (or not damaging) themselves; therefore this feverish activism is transformed, as seen from both the individual characters' inner selves and from the whole of society, into a completely ossified human passivity. In objective social terms, there comes into being the apparatus desired by Stalin, an apparatus in which all instructions from "above", as in every good machine, tend to be implemented without friction. Because of this, the executive organ seems to be degraded into a cog in the machine. Yet when considered so abstractly, this is merely an illusion. For a complete devotion to a common social activity and a voluntary and total submission to its requirements need not necessarily have an unfavourable effect on human development. Should an individual decide to subordinate himself unconditionally to the whole, and if this decision is based on a genuine, subjectively honest, indeed passionate conviction that the goals of this whole will benefit humanity, then such a commitment might well, admittedly in a paradoxical and problematic way, also benefit his personality. Such cases are not very common even in revolutionary times, but various hybrid forms of this attitude are very common indeed. Only the absolute priority of mere tactical decisions, springing from an egoism governed by hope and fear restricts such a man to the narrow confines of his own particular being, and reduces him in fact to an anonymous cog in the great machine. The dialectic of bureaucratic activism revealed here makes men static and passive; it transforms their cleverly thought-out decisions into the monotonous incapacity for human development.

In the case of many victims of the bureaucratic internment system, this dialectical interaction between man and society has the reverse effect. However abstractly uniform all decrees may be in themselves, whenever they are applied to individual cases they must be made into concrete decrees concerning individual people, and here extremely individual countermovements can arise. For how and whether an individual human being survives or perishes in the degrading and bureaucratically favourable or punitive order of the camps depends on extremely fine shades of individual reactions. For example, how and whether certain acts of adaptation, which objectively are difficult to avoid, react upon those adapting to them naturally depends largely on what is required of them, but in the final analysis on how they can personally accomplish and internalize the necessary adaptation. And this attempt to decribe the contradictory nature of such processes does far less than justice to their complexity. For the individual always bases his decisions on a certain social situation; his decisions depend principally on the idea he has of society, of his position in it and of his attitude towards it, as well as on the commandments that because of this position he regards as binding, etc.

To be sure, the camp leaders make demands which can only be answered negatively if a man wishes to preserve his humanity at all. As the extreme, one might mention spying or testifying against fellow sufferers, which is incessantly demanded by the apparatus. Those who are weak or cowardly submit without resistance to such pressure. More complicated is the situation of those inmates who, even under these circumstances, retain their communist convictions, their sense of belonging to the Party. Solzhenitsyn shows cases fundamentally different from one another. The Communist, Rubin, about whom we must say more later, at first sharply rejects such demands. This man, who had fought in the war, replies to the Security Officer of the camp police force with: "Well, I've proved my loyalty to the Soviet regime in blood, so I don't have to prove it in ink as well."[5] When the same officer summons him again, he veils his refusal somwhat more "diplomatically" by interpreting his remark thus: ". . . Rubin excused himself on the obviously false pretext that, since he was in prison, he was evidently regarded as politically un-

[5]Ibid, p. 178

reliable, and so long as this was so, he could not *collaborate* with the head of security."[6]

Since then, of course, he is in disfavour, and incriminating material is constantly collected against him. In the case of the youth, Doronin, whom the authorities do recruit, in addition to inexperience and the fear of being transferred back to the old camp, ideological factors are at work: the mockery of all moral categories such as "goodness" and "conscience", and in his youth, the praise of denunciation as a patriotic duty; all this has not been without its effect on him. He allows himself to be recruited. To be sure, he does attempt a ruse by initiating his most important fellow prisoners into his intention of ferreting out the authorities' plans, but this attempt at "tactically" outsmarting the officials very soon proves to be worthless. Here every real compromise must lead to a loss of human dignity. A refusal to compromise in all human and social essentials thus forms a pre-requisite for anyone wishing to remain really human in the camps. Naturally this attitude has extremely varied ramifications: the one indispensable condition is only that something be involved which in one way or another points beyond the merely particular, for only such forces—which, viewed from the standpoint of particularity, appear imaginary—can create a lasting desire for self-preservation and a genuine resistance in the individual in the face of pressures which otherwise appear irresistible. The concrete gradations of actual individual resistance are innumerable; they are varied individually in each individual. However, since over decades the struggle for human self-preservation can daily, at times even hourly, put every man to serious tests, human reserves of a merely subjective character are useless in igniting such a permanently self-renewing counter-movement and in sustaining the characters continuously at such a level. They must be sustained by some general, socio-human set of values, even though they may be

[6] Loc. cit. (italics in original)

incapable of realization at the moment. Only the influence of such values, constantly reacting on the characters, in a continuous interaction with the moral and intellectual conditioning factors of the people concerned, is able to bring the individual to the point of resistance and induce him to stand fast.

Since the "first circle" is filled predominantly with learned specialists, scholarship, objectivity, purity of thought, etc. naturally play a dominant role in such relationships—of course frequently in a lively interrelation with a scholarly egoism. That these are the foundations of inner life is very clear in figures such as Sologdin. For him "not knuckling under" stands at the centre of his whole existence; his motto is: "A man has to school himself to develop unshakeable will-power and subordinate it to his reason."[7] For Sologdin, the objective completion of mental labour, which expresses itself as an affirmation of the "law of the last inch" and as patience, stubbornness and self-criticism in the service of true perfectionism, shields him from the pressing practical consequences of his own activity. And in this he can also give free reign to the egoism of his social status. Because of this, he becomes the model, almost the teacher of outstanding people such as Nerzhin, and also because of this there is for him no "better" place than prison "to understand the part of good and evil in human life".[8] This is why he is engaged in continuous ironical quarrel with the convinced Communist, Rubin (to be sure, a mutual human sympathy does exist between them). Among the surprising and amusing episodes of this monotony, with its hidden underlying drama, is a vehement discussion about dialectics (of course in the then predominant Stalinist form) which breaks out between the two. It is of no importance here that their understanding of the dialectic is equally sound, but that nevertheless for different reasons, neither is

[7] *Ibid.*, p. 219
[8] *Ibid.*, p. 169

able to grasp its true problems; the important thing is only that for Sologdin the rejection, and for Rubin the defence of the existing dialectics remain the decisive issue of their spiritual and moral existence in the camp. Thus Rubin comes incessantly into inner conflict. For friendship is for him an indispensable part of life, and here he cannot befriend like-minded persons, while all his friends reject his views. In spite of this, communication remains a vital necessity for him; in order to be able to exist accordingly, he repeatedly recites humorous parodies of poems (Moses, Igorli), the only effect of which is that he must subsequently be ashamed of the role that he has played.

This factor is more important than it at first appears. For it illuminates the other side of what we have until now been able to establish as characteristic of the moral elite among the prisoners. We have established a contrast between the camp authorities and the inmates: in the former we observed the dehumanized passivity that constitutes the core of their incessant and feverish, if often tactically adroit activity; in the latter, in this group of "human objects" we find that behind their imposed impotence and behind their passivity of forced obedience there is a self-chosen *praxis*—the inextinguishable inner activity of a humanity defending itself. This contrast must be decisive in every comparison between the two groups. However, it only characterizes the abstract and general nature of the human substance of the intellectually and morally outstanding prisoners; this substance itself can only be really understood if one also makes its specific contrasts plainly visible. We must therefore return for a moment to the figure of Sologdin. Just as in Rubin's attitude an obvious tendency toward the eccentric can be recognized without difficulty, so too is there a similar tendency in Sologdin's puritanical intellectual attitude. He demands and practises, as we have seen, an unrelenting and uncompromising uniformity of thought; so that alongside principles of behaviour of which we may approve, we find, for instance his over-anxious avoidance of all words of foreign origin, which he sees as "bird words" and believes to be pretentious: instead of scepticism he says "all-embracing doubt", instead of method, "a bird's eye view of the approach to work", etc. And he is sincerely filled with shame when on one occasion the term "sphere" slips out.[9] Now what else is this but a whim of an eccentric?

Of course in purely psychological terms one is used to regarding eccentricity, or the making of unimportant whims into the point around which life revolves, as a psychic peculiarity of certain people. This approach is wrong, especially here. For eccentricity is a certain attitude on the part of the subject which arises from the specific nature of reality and the potentiality of his own social *praxis*. More precisely, it arises from the fact that a character may well be inwardly capable of denying certain forms of the society in which he is forced to live, and indeed those very forms which are decisive for the conduct of his personal and moral life, in such a way that his inner integrity (which they threaten) remains intact; however, the conversion of this rejection into a really individual *praxis* (which has now become necessary for his humanity) is rendered impossible by society and therefore he must remain enmeshed in a more or less abstractly distorted inwardness. In this process his character acquires crotchety eccentricity. In order to comprehend the relationship between the individual and society in this special case, this type must above all be distinguished from the cynically humorous depravity which often stands at a high intellectual level, and which also originates in the social situation. Neither Falstaff nor Rameau's Nephew are eccentrics. They do not possess this morally motivated resistance. They adapt, but at the same time they criticize shrewdly

[9] *Ibid.*, p. 171

the society that demands such an adaptation of them, and they criticize themselves because their adaptation is based on egoism.

Eccentricity is essentially a modern phenomenon, the product of the first really socialized society, namely of capitalism. Don Quixote's comical grandeur, which has never been surpassed, is on the borderline. It originates pre-eminently in a misguided heroism; it is the great rearguard action of the best moral qualities of a decaying feudal world. Remote relationship to the eccentric arises only because each of his honest and heroic struggles ends in grotesque comedy, and because his moral core, the sustaining force of his inflexible personality, must, whenever he attempts to realize it, give the lie to itself through comedy. However, Don Quixote's *praxis*—and thus his personality as well—is here unbroken, both in subjective and objective terms. By contrast, eccentricity from Sterne to Dickens and Raabe originates precisely in the power of society to react upon and deform the subject, in the fact that personality and society are not able to hold each other in check. In this way the most honest and most warranted resistance is objectively distorted into eccentricity, though subjectively integrity need not founder on it.

In Nerzhin's case this attitude appears in a more subtle form. Learning and understanding were already his passions in early youth. He follows the trial of the engineers with huge doubts; and he no longer believes a word of the reports of the trials of the old Bolsheviks. After he reads Lenin, Stalin's content and style seem to him—as he remarks on one occasion to Stalin's admirer, Rubin—to be a mess. "Every thing Stalin says is crude and stupid—he always misses the most important point."[10] Thus he went to war, and from war into prison. Learning and understanding remain his guiding stars here too. And although in his former free life he had been a gifted mathematician, he now has a vital interest only

[10] *Ibid.*, p. 52

in human destiny. He reflects on historical problems, but must of course carefully conceal his notes. Thus it happens that, when his old professor recommends him for a job which holds the prospect of a release ahead of time and a pardon, he says openly: "No . . . Let them admit first that it is not right to put people in prison for their way of thinking—and then *we* will see whether we can forgive them."[11] When, following this conversation, his superior in fact makes the offer, he declines, of course more "diplomatically", by giving reasons which refer to the demands of his present duties. Naturally his desire to continue his secret historical studies also plays an important role. He thus acts in quite a different way in a crucial situation to Sologdin. This resolute devotion to problems of humanity (on one occasion, filled with enthusiasm, he analyses *Faust*, again in a conversation with Rubin) determines his relations with "the people": a healthy plebeian attitude is for him the only worthy basis for a relation to human beings and their community. In the circumstances, however, this deep conviction must remain a mere feeling; translated into deeds, it appears eccentric. Nerzhin's one active self-expression in the course of the novel is his real friendship with the peasant, Spiridon, in whom he sees the embodiment of "the people", precisely because Spiridon's life, abundantly filled with blows of fate, again and again gives rise to the questions which cannot be answered by his view of life. Not that these questions are too complicated or deep; rather because Spiridon always acts on the basis of his simple peasant instincts, often cleverly and adroitly, never losing his human genuineness, and yet always, for good or evil, without regard to what the social rationale of his decision could be (e.g. he changes over without conflict from the White partisans to the Reds, at first becomes a victim of the new collective farm system and later eagerly assists its construction.) Now almost blind, he lives in the camp, and when Nerzhin, after listening to him for a

[11] *Ibid.*, p. 60

long time, asks: who is right? who is guilty? Spiridon answers with unshakable certainty: "Sheepdogs are right and cannibals are wrong."[12] Here too it is important for the sake of clarity to separate Spiridon's attitude from that of his intellectual admirer. In the former case, there is not a trace of eccentricity. Subjectively and humanly considered, his nature has reached the extreme of what Marx used to call ignorant perfection. However, enthusiasm for a human ideal of this type, in the case of such a versatile and sagacious person as Nerzhin, doubtless points to eccentricity. All the more so since, despite his admiration, he is necessarily unable to apply this peasant wisdom in even an intellectually practical way; on the contrary, it neither provides a foundation for nor enlarges his mental world, but rather it objectively confuses and distorts it. This peasant wisdom does give him the appearance of having a firm foundation, a broader perspective, and in Nerzhin both these are subjectively authentic to a high degree. However, when he must take a stand on questions important to him, his decision, based on deeply felt convictions, has nothing in common with either Spiridon's practical way of life or with his "theoretical" wisdom which Nerzhin so admires. Nerzhin remains attached to Spiridon, but without the remotest possibility of realizing his theoretical wisdom in practice (even on an intellectual level). One must therefore, and we shall return to this point later, always perceive and pay heed to the valuable latent forces (even if they are merely ignorant perfection) residing in the common people, but at the same time one must clearly distinguish between two different views of them. The first sees in the ignorant perfection of "the people's" life huge reserve human forces which, once their ignorance is overcome, could be developed into powerful vehicles of their revolutionary re-birth. The second stops at a mere uncritical admiration of the forces of unity of the people—"the humblest man can be perfect" says Goethe—

[12] *Ibid.*, p. 486

and thus generally lapses into eccentricity, as Nerzhin does here. We intentionally said "generally", for when a critique of an existing civilization confronts that civilization with the latent forces of the people's life, it can endow its art with the pathos of a devastating accusation; it is sufficient to mention Bartok's *Cantata Profana*. But in that case the admiration of the common people is converted into an active, plebeian, revolutionary indictment which in art and above all in music, does not need a goal capable of concrete realization in order to signpost the vital areas of human life. For Nerzhin there is naturally no way out; this is why the tendencies which are in any case within him develop into eccentricity.

The conclusion of the novel brings only two, long awaited, events: Volodin is arrested and Nerzhin is transported to an ordinary internment camp. The rich and variegated light thrown on the inner life of an epoch (the era of Stalin's last years, following the break with Tito) produces no real changes, either subjectively in the characters or objectively in society. The action is strictly limited to revealing what is happening at that precise time. It is thus no accident that this rich complex of human reactions needs only a few days in which to unfold. This short period is sufficient to develop those reactions to their logical conclusion.

3.

The second novel takes place during a more troubled period, namely after Stalin's death, at the time of the initial attempts at coming to terms with his legacy: its "setting" which triggers the human reactions is a cancer ward in the depth of the provinces. The confrontations it generates are not the same as those of its predecessor: it is about—and here it is closer to *The Magic Mountain*—the condition between life and death, about life in the shadow of death, about the significance of an imminent death for the characters' way of life. This introduces a completely new group of characters with important functions of action and reaction, a group which is directly connected neither actively nor passively with the politics of the Stalin era, and which can thus represent the broad, non-involved masses of the employed who were confronted with such problem complexes—which could not be done in the first novel. Moreover, the majority of the patients who have lived normal lives are also called upon to resolve these dilemmas. This is not to imply that the central significance of the great contrast in the first novel disappears or is superseded. The time of the action alone makes this impossible. And in fact here too interest focuses on the same polar opposites, but in accordance with the change in place and time, the contrast between them is extended and intensified.

However, by making these polar opposites stand out against a broad canvas and by constructing a situation in which problems arising from the threat of death are complicated by the specific features inherent in life during the Stalinist period Solzhenitsyn has produced a novel which is very closely related to the First Circle, and not merely because of the similarities in the narrative form.

Let us begin with the new group of characters. It ranges from the patients without convictions for political crimes to the personnel of the hospital, the doctors (who are predominantly women) and nurses. Even when one reads the two novels only superficially, it strikes one that nowhere is there a figure whose thoughts and feelings are even remotely concerned with a restoration, with the overthrow of the socialist regime to say nothing of the re-introduction of capitalism. In the first novel, a superficial reader could perhaps trace this back to the feeling of being observed and to the suppression of secret thoughts. Here, where the majority of characters can move about freely and lead uncontrolled private lives,

Solzhenitsyn's view of contemporary reality is clearly manifest.

It would have been worthwhile to describe the personnel of the hospital more precisely than is possible here. It goes without saying that the material possibilities are extremely limited; it also goes without saying that the external order is governed by a bureaucraticism that can very easily manifest itself as inhumanity, e.g. as regulations compelling the ward to send hopeless cases home to die so that their beds can be freed for new admissions. Still, it is often shown how the doctors fight on behalf of every patient and at times even force the bureaucracy to beat a retreat. Even more important, however, is their attitude, in their overwhelming majority, to the patients. The psychology of the majority is far removed from any deadening routine and from any "scientific" arrogance which might see the patients as guinea pigs to be used for the progress of research (and thus of their own careers). On the contrary, their research and their methodological self-criticism are overwhelmingly in the service of curing, which of course is here extremely rare. For the chief doctor, Donsova, self-examination culminates in the fact that she soon forgets all "her best cases, her hardest-won victories, but until the day she dies she would always remember the handful of poor devils who had fallen under the wheels."[13] Kostoglotov, who takes up a critical attitude on all human questions, says of the doctor Vera Hangart that she is not kind as a matter of duty, but simply because she is a good person. And the author himself remembers of the chief doctor Donsova, who has genuine talent and a passion for research, that she has none of the weaknesses which could advance her scientific career. For this reason, the patients, in their various ways, regard her with an unshakable respect. Her clever sympathetic understanding and insight cause

[13] Alexander Solzhenitsyn, *Cancer Ward*, Vol. I (London, The Bodley Head Ltd., 1968), p. 105

Kostoglotov, who is rapidly improving and who would like
to leave the hospital in order to realize his extremely dubious
prospects in life in his own way, to stay on and continue the
cure which he has begun. Her knowledge; her discerning
human superiority triumphs over the wilfulness with which
he protests against the doctors' right to decide their patients'
fate without the latter's consent and declares that he does not
want to be saved at any price. Her clear-sighted decisiveness,
which in the final analysis is lovable because it is based on
human kindness, overcome his eccentric obstinacy. The con-
ceited bureaucrat, Rusanov, who here feels himself socially
degraded and who wishes to be treated only in an elegant
hospital in the city, must also yield to her wise determina-
tion.

Thus we are shown an entire group of characters who
know little of the arbitrary horrors of the practice of internment, and who have remained unaffected by them in their
personal lives—Donsova is extremely surprised, indeed is
angered and shaken to the point of incomprehension when
she hears Kostoglotov tell of the initial treatment of his disease
at the time of his deportation. It is revealed at the same time
how that which we called eccentricity on the part of the
morally best inmates does not originate in some inherent
psychological inclination, but rather is the distorting effect
of the way of life forced upon them, their brave resistance
to it and their successful attempt at preserving their own
human integrity even here. These doctors in the cancer ward
do not exhibit any eccentric traits whatever.

These are also absent in the patients when the consequences
of the disease's progress change into human drama. Thus the
gay young girl, Asya, who until then has been unconcerned,
learns that her breast is to be operated on and removed. She
runs in despair to her devoted admirer, the high school
student Dyoma, who has recently had his leg amputated. She
sees her future life as completely hopeless: who would still

want her when she had only one breast? She scarcely hears
Dyoma's attempts at consolation—he himself is still confined
to bed—and his declaration that he will marry her all the
same. "How will I be able to go to the beach?" she cries, and
finally she bares her breast so that Dyoma can be the last to
see and kiss it.[14] Much more significant tragic action is initiated
when the chief doctor, Donsova discovers that she herself is
suffering from cancer. Her suppressed despair and her brave
absence of illusion present us with the picture of a noble
woman who endeavours to integrate her own death sentence
into an attitude to life that preserves her humanity.

But even on the level of purely theoretical conversation the
differences between the characters here and the eccentrics in
the camp is clearly expressed. The young scholar, Vadim,
who is gifted but immature, speaks of the interest scientific
problems hold for him. The seriously ill Shulubin, who has
also not been imprisoned, and whom we must later discuss
at greater length, sternly rejects mere interest as a motive
for scholarship. "If that's your explanation science becomes
no different from the ordinary run of selfish, thoroughly
unethical occupations,"[15] and, using seemingly trivial examples
based on everyday experiences, he points to science's function
of transforming real life in a human sense and claims that
what one does with it is what makes it really valuable. Quite
apart from rightness or wrongness, neither one bases his argument on an eccentric position.

By contrast, from Kostoglotov's story we learn of a doctor
who lives and works in the same village in the Steppes, having
been exiled there for life. With indescribable difficulty, the
ageing gynaecologist, Kadmin, is able to arrange for his wife,
who has also been exiled, to live there with him. They build
for themselves an harmonious, even happy life. He is loved
and respected by the people; he can even call a cottage with

[14] *Ibid.*, Vol. II, pp.120-21
[15] *Ibid.*, p. 102

a garden his own and, quoting Korolenko, can feel comfortable because the external order ensures inner peace. Thus they create their own order: in the garden there are no useful plants which would make them self-sufficient—"but you can buy all those things" say the Kadmins[16]—and although they do keep animals, they again reject all that is practical in a small village: cows, pigs, chickens, etc., and instead own only dogs and cats with whom they develop almost human bonds. Kostoglotov forms a deep attachment to the Kadmins and their dogs and cats; if possible he would like to move from the cancer ward into this village with a doctor and nurse, in order to live out the remnants of his life in as human a way as possible.

Here again we see how the best of the inmates can normally salvage their human dignity only in eccentric ways and for themselves alone. Kostoglotov has acquired a clearer insight into the bases of his own intellectual and moral existence than have most of those who share his fate. "To be frank, I'm not much of a clinger to life. It's not only that there's none ahead of me, there's none behind me either."[17] The difficulty of life in internment, devoid of perspective, combined with an insight into the hopelessness of his disease determine both his eccentricity and a dawning suspicion that it is rooted in his existence. The specific nature of his life is both internally and externally determined. Despite the passion of his individual attitudes, he is far more a receptive type than an innovating or creative one. Characteristically, he quotes a saying of his grandfather, "A fool loves to teach, but a clever man loves to learn."[18] This is naturally determined to a large extent by his fate: deportation has terminated his studies and he is already too old to be able to catch up on what he has missed even if he should be pardoned. Still, he passionately acquires

[16] *Ibid.*, Vol. I, p. 318
[17] *Ibid.*, p. 92
[18] *Ibid.*, p. 137

any accessible knowledge of reality, but lacks any ideas (or illusion) of how this knowledge might be used productively in the future. A destiny like that of his doctor friend is the maximum that he still desires in life.

Of course the change in social existence from that of "the first circle" plays a role in this behaviour. There, the immutability and so the fixed and total hopelessness of the period of the last few years of Stalin's life formed the determining context. Now, however, it seems that a decisive change is about to take place. It is of course characteristic of cumulative effects of the past that only Kostoglotov and the bureaucrat Rusanov really want to see the newspapers which report it. Although the news of the impending change (the deposing of Malenkov) passionately excites Kostoglotov, he can no longer change his essential attitude to life.

Completely opposite, but in their way just as typical, are Rusanov's reactions to these social changes. We know that, inwardly raging, he adjusted to being treated in such an ordinary hospital and among such commonplace people. When the newspaper is brought daily, he is also outraged that Kostoglotov does not respect his priority. He is the only one, so he thinks, who is able to read a newspaper correctly. For him it is "a widely distributed instruction written in fact in code; nothing in it could be said openly but a skilful man who knew the ropes could interpret the various small hints, the arrangement of articles, the things that were played down or omitted, and so get a true picture of the way things were going."[19] But it is all too understandable that the patently obvious symptoms of a fundamental change of climate invoke in Rusanov a panic combined with indignation. This is first of all manifest in a nightmare in which individual victims of his denunciations appear; he is summoned before the new Supreme Court, although he is deeply convinced that he has acted correctly and that he has done nothing more than carry out his "simple duty

[19] *Ibid.*, p. 245

71

as a citizen."[20] Thus he now lives in a permanent atmosphere of fear until his daughter comes to visit him from the capital.

She is worthy of him. It will not surprise the reader that Solzhenitsyn should paint a satirical caricature of her. Unfortunately, like other extreme caricatures of people who are conformists to the point of self-annihilation, this one also begins to degenerate into an artistic stereotype. Even Rusanov's daughter is basically outraged at the current change of climate. "All right," she says, "granted it was a long time ago they convicted those people rightly or wrongly . . . but why bring them back now?" This, in her opinion, is a "painful, agonizing process."[21] In general people active in the immediate past are treated unjustly: "A man who 'sends a signal' is being politically conscious and progressive."[22] She adds of course that ". . . you have to be responsive to the demand of the times . . . whether or not we like it . . ."[23] At the same time she shows that, if one only has the right connections and knows how to use them properly, all these difficulties can be overcome; one must only . . . have tact and be responsive to the times." This is "the vital thing."[24] With pride, with growing reassurance, Rusanov regards the daughter who is so worthy of him. She, having just given up journalism for literature in Moscow, contributes her views on matters of principle, and thus arouses the interest of those present in the room. She treats the idea of ideological volte-face with mildly superior scorn: ". . . they used to say 'There must be no conflict'. But now they talk about 'the false theory of the absence of conflict.' . . . but when everyone starts talking the new way all at once, you don't notice there's been a transition at all."[25] Thus while she mocks people like Yevtushenko with

[20] *Ibid.*, p. 253
[21] *Ibid.*, p. 326
[22] *Ibid.*, p. 327
[23] *Ibid.*, p. 329
[24] *Ibid.*, p. 333
[25] *Ibid.*, p. 332-33

an air of superiority, she summarizes the new ideology in such a way that no one can distinguish it from the literary dogmas of the heyday of Stalinism. ". . . one may describe the good things quite fearlessly, so as to make them even better."[26] To describe something that exists is much more simple than to describe something that does not yet exist but which doubtlessly will exist one day. "Truth is what we *must* be, what is going to happen tomorrow. . . ."[27] Of course she tactfully does not employ the Zhdanovian romantic terminology, but very likely considers it the central point of the current requirements. Rusanov can be reassured; his daughter will successfully take up where he left off.

With this meeting Rusanov regains his old assurance; he feels that he will successfully come to terms with the new era, with all its changes which preserve the essential methods of Stalinism with only superficial modifications. Shortly after this, when his son comes to visit him, he speaks with all the assurance of his old routine, and calls his attention to *his* "mistakes" (or deviations from the inhuman bureaucratic schematism). For this reason he can much more easily come to terms with his own existence in the hospital, and understands that one must treat even "an insignificant little nurse" with diplomatic caution if one wishes to avoid any unpleasantness. Outbreaks of anger at the bad new days do not seriously impair his sense of well-being, which admittedly is connected with a perhaps temporary improvement in his physical condition. When on Stalin's birthday a very ordinary article without photographs or extravagant eulogy appears in the newspaper, he is for a moment beside himself: ". . . what remains? What can one rely on?"[28] he exclaims. However the possibility of smooth adaptation to a reality unchanged in its essential nature remains the stronger motive in his thoughts

[26] *Ibid.*, p. 336
[27] *Ibid.*, p. 337
[28] *Ibid.*, Vol. II, p. 23

and actions. Solzhenitsyn again shows correctly, truly and typically the unchanging psychology of a bureaucratically paralysed conservatism which adjusts to everything.

On the other hand, these events provoke intense outbursts of indignation, hitherto suppressed. Thus Kostoglotov again explodes when he hears of a swindler who, through clever manoeuvring, has evaded the consequences of his misdeeds by making a timely declaration of repentance, a case which Rusanov praises as a sign of the system's humanity. The milder critics see in this a remnant of bourgeois consciousness. But Kostoglotov is quite beside himself. According to him it is simply a matter of human greed which existed before bourgeois society and will exist after it. The vigorous defence of this thesis then leads him to brand as a kind of racism the custom of exploiting one's proletarian origin to obtain privileges. Although his arguments are often sophisticated and factually untenable, again and again they are seen to be rooted in a genuine plebeian hatred of social privilege: "It makes no difference if you had ten proletarian grandfathers, if you're not a worker yourself you're no proletarian! . . . He's not a proletarian, he's a son of a bitch. The only thing he's after is a special pension . . ."[29] Kostoglotov receives unexpected help from Shulubin who recalls the April Theses (1917) according to which an official's salary—corresponding to the model of the 1871 Commune—ought not to be higher than the average pay of a good worker.

Shortly thereafter there follows Shulubin's long-suppressed self-critical and socially-critical confession. Apart from reprimands and slights, he had led a normal, "free" life and had been neither arrested nor imprisoned during the great period of crisis. Now he reports the human price he had to pay for being spared: "You haven't had to do much lying, do you understand? At least you haven't had to stoop so low—you should appreciate that! You people were arrested,

[29] *Ibid.*, p. 134

but we were herded into meetings to 'expose' you. They executed people like you, but they made us stand up and applaud the verdicts as they were announced. And not just applaud, they made us demand the firing squad, *demand* it!"[30] Kostoglotov has a spontaneous sympathy for this outburst of moral despair. It all depends, he says, on the number one drew. He himself might perhaps have been a member of the choir like Shulubin, and the latter would have endured deportation just as he had. The conversation then ranges far beyond this confession. Shulubin passionately rejects the occasional condemnation of socialism, and especially any tolerance of bourgeois society voiced by his interlocutor. Although he is sceptical about a democratization of socialism, he does profess to believe in an "ethical socialism", which he concretizes with reference to the names of Vladimir Solovyov and Kropotkin. Apart from the critique of the Stalinist system, the conversation does not make clear what Solzhenitsyn himself thinks of the social and human value of such tendencies; we do not know whether he merely thinks them characteristic of Shulubin or regards them as a real solution.

4.

From the point of view of the development of the novel, Solzhenitsyn's two works mark him as an exceptionally gifted exponent of the new method whose beginnings we dated from *The Magic Mountain*. We see immediately how the individual characters react to the stimuli of society and how, despite the dominance of a particular social tendency and the place they occupy in it, they achieve in their personal lives a maximum of sensuous clarity and of intellectual and moral self-

[30] *Ibid.*, p. 164

awareness. Solzhenitsyn's achievement is not at all diminished by the fact that in his portrayal of bureaucratic inhumanity he sometimes produces over-schematic and abstract types. At the same time, however, it becomes apparent that just because individual reactions appear fortuitous and just because they are only loosely (or not at all) connected with the plot, the whole created world achieves an unparalleled perfection, above all in its portrayal of the contradictions inherent in it. So it is no accident that Solzhenitsyn has selected this narrative method in order to depict an historically extremely important transitional period in humanity's path to socialism, emphasizing particularly its profound contradictions and its only too obvious negative features.

The crucial point here is the revelation of the essential structure of the immanent contradictions of that period—Hegel rightly speaks of the unity of unity and contradiction, rather than simply defining unity as the centre of the dialectical method as the best way of making oneself and others aware of a period and its dynamic, manifold, internal and external complexity. This unity of the unity and diversity, which as a rule is heightened into antithesis, yields a correct picture of what really has to be overcome in such a transition. Which of Solzhenitsyn's impressions of reality and experiences in writing and thinking have contributed to this artistic clarity is of secondary interest. For the richness of his creative method, which we outlined briefly at the outset, consists precisely in the fact that its ultimate ordering principle—in content and in form—enables it to assimilate the most diverse subjects and distortions of them. It is "only" necessary that the writer begin with the dynamic unity of his subject matter and not with an abstract principle of form "applied" to this subject matter. If in the context of world literature, Solzhenitsyn's works appear as a rebirth of the noble beginnings of socialist realism, then objectively inherent in this concept of rebirth is the dialectical unity of continuity and

discontinuity; and it is also of secondary importance to discover which subjective elements have inspired, and stimulated
this rebirth in Solzhenitsyn's creative works. One way or
another, he has discovered the right form for his artistic
purposes.

The mere statement, however, that these novels represent
a large-scale continuation of the past flowering of socialist
realism does not do justice to the problem of their significance
in the present. One cannot avoid the question of whether
and to what degree such works are political novels. However,
if we are really in search of an answer, then we must begin
with the contemporary socio-intellectual situation, a subject
about which there is the greatest imaginable confusion.
According to the new current in the Stalinist period, the
political character of literature became manifest in its obliga-
tion to provide definite and concrete guidlines for the solution
of certain current political problems; its value or lack of
value depended upon whether and to what extent these
solutions were able to pave the way for correct political
decisions in practical life. The essential criterion of this cor-
rectness was not difficult to specify at the time: it was the
latest resolution of the appropriate political authority; if this
resolution was changed while the work concerned was in
progress, then the characters and their fates had to be re-
worked so that they were now suited to support the new
resolution. Thus the re-interpretation of the partisan nature
of literature turned out to be no more than a formal con-
formity to party decrees. The document which allegedly
establishes this theory does not at all refer to imaginative
literature. (Lenin's well-known essay of 1905; cf. Krupskaya's
letter), and the artistic quality of the works produced by this
method was terrifyingly bad (the fate of Fadeyev's *Young
Guard* comes to mind) but neither of those factors was able
to drive the regulations out of theory and practice.

In such cases it is always advisable to refer back to Marx

himself. In his preface to *A Contribution to the Critique of Political Economy*, he says of ideology in general: Ideological forms (art included) are, when conflicts arise socially and objectively, the medium "in which men become conscious of this conflict and fight it out."[31] It has become a habit to conceive, without reference to Marx, the momentary ideology of an era as something primarily uniform from which the particular and individual ideological standpoints are then derived and differentiated logically. But it is often forgotten that Marx—not by chance, we believe—lists the most important ideological forms whose findings on matters within their competence are expressed in forms applicable to this struggle. Henceforth that which we may call the ideology of a period rightly originates (subsequently, not *a priori*) in the synthesis, completed in and through *praxis*, of various ideological decisions, in various fields, by various classes, etc. Until now only Lenin has given an adequate interpretation, and that for politics: the task of politics as an ideology, he says, is, in a critical period of transition, to recognize and understand the link in the chain which, when seized, places a person (politician, party, class, etc.) in a position to grasp and control the whole chain.

But can this direct relation to social *praxis* be the sole form in which this "fighting out" in Marx's sense is realized for all ideologies? To remain only with art and with fiction, writings whose main purpose consists in, e.g., bringing about the removal of a paragraph from the statute-book or the addition of a new paragraph to the old, are produced constantly and in large quantities. After several thousand years' experience, one might ask whether this is the central ideological task of fiction. A serious survey of the history of fiction from Homer to Makarenko or Thomas Mann, would doubtless lead to a quite different conclusion. For here we see

[31] M & E Selected works, Vol. I., p. 329, Moscow 1951

that the link to be seized is man, together with the prevailing social conditions and tendencies, as determined by and determining the change in society. The central question that is raised and answered becomes: how do such social factors influence man? Do they strengthen or inhibit him in his historical mission to achieve the social development of the humanization of man? Solzhenitsyn's significance as novelist rests above all on the fact that he gives clear and convincing compendia of the inhibiting after-effects of the Stalinist period.

Is this political? The answer is, directly, hardly at all, but indirectly to a high degree. Without question, nowhere does he so much as hint at a "link in the chain", the seizing of which could strengthen or demolish this system. Yet on the other hand tranformations which take place in his heroes as we have seen, are so unnerving that anyone who is sensitive to literture or who is deeply concerned with human fate can be initiated into the process of making political decisions by such reading matter. But it is a question—and this is the essence and limit of artistic effect—of a potential "Can", never, even only in intent, of an unconditional "Must".

Thus when Solzhenitsyn denies having written with political goals in mind, and when on the other hand writers hostile to him compare his novels with the biased, and ignorant directly politically intended babble of Stalin's daughter, their criticism can readily be rejected as slander. However, Solzhenitsyn's statements about the meaning of his own works are unclear to the extent that his works are surely just as political in the final analysis as are those of Beaumarchais or Diderot, Goethe or Tolstoy. In order to grasp the complexity of this situation we must bear in mind both that Goethe's *Werther* is far from being unpolitical and the *The Marriage of Figaro* was not one of the political forces which unleashed the French Revolution. The struggle against true realist literature was senseless and ineffective in the *Lettres de Cachet* and in Tolstoy's excommunication, just as at the other pole the canonization of Goethe as an Olympian enthroned far above all political struggles did not correspond to the facts. Solzhenitsyn's persistent opponents read into his works far-fetched political ideas and credit them with great political impact; but he would delude himself if he really felt that his writings, which in fact are aimed at a comprehensive portrayal of people in this era, had no relation whatever to the important political decisions of the present day. Such political implications appear more or less indirectly, depending on the work, but they cannot possibly be excluded from the attempts of individuals to constitute themselves in the struggle raging round the Stalinist heritage.

This indirect relation is by no means lacking in aesthetic implications for the works themselves. Without drawing or wanting to draw directly political conclusions, such pictures of human reactions to social structures and tendencies have various levels of profundity, of insight into the nature of the forces here at work, of their influence on human develop-ment or alienation, on the human means of making operative that which is favourable and overcoming or re-shaping the unfavourable. Here too, one should not precipitately identify the abstract content, which naturally can always be inter-preted politically, with the artistic substance which is primarily though often indirectly related to human types. The level referred to here has at its foundation the truthful, comprehensive, accurate description of both the objective and subjective tendencies at work at the moment, and thus determines immediately the ultimate truth of the literary product.

When, for example in *The Magic Mountain* Thomas Mann makes Castorp volunteer for the First World War and presents this as the subjective conclusion of all his intellectual and moral adventures, this does not nearly exhaust the ideologi-cally and socially founded artistic truth of his work. Only

when Castorp's deliberations are again made actual for us in
the loneliness of his experience in the snowstorm do we
approach the artistic truth of the work.. In that scene both
the competing figures and their ideological-political contest
become actual for Castorp. About Settembrini he thinks:
"You are a braggart and a hand-organ man, but you mean well,
you mean much better and more to my mind than that knife-
edged little Jesuit and Terrorist, apologist of the Inquisition
and the knout, with his round eye-glasses—though he
is nearly always right when you and he come to grips . . ."[32]
Translated into general, concrete social terms, what does this
mean? That the liberal burgher, Castorp can have genuinely
human sympathies—to be sure, not without ironical reservations—for such an honest representative of his own political
ideology, but at the same time feels strongly that this standpoint is not intellectually defensible against such a sophisticated attack from modern reaction. Castorp thus goes to war
to defend his old Germany, but sees that the "power-protected
inwardness" of people like him is defenceless against attacks
from the right. This represents the most profound and comprehensive artistic achievement on the part of the German
bourgeoisie before the victory of fascism, in a situation in
which the question is put to it on an undeveloped level, namely
on the level of its position towards the war. Is such a literary
insight political? The answer can be Yes only in our sense of a
mediation which is frequently very remote, since between the
artistic level of this portrayal and its indirect effect actual
social connections do exist, but are distantly mediated.

This constellation is even more evident in Tolstoy's works.
This is for us all the more interesting, since the latter is ideologically connected with Solzhenitsyn through the leading
role which the plebeian social view of the portrayed
characters, human fates and human relations plays in the

[32] *The Magic Mountain*, Ch. 6, "Snow" (London, Secker & Warburg, 1957, trans. H. T. Lowe-Porter), p. 478.

works of both. (It is no accident that in the *Cancer Ward* discussions about the actual value to life of Tolstoy's book, *What Men Live By*, play a not insignificant role.) In both the sharp contrast between plebeian (in essence: peasant-plebeian) principles of life and the forms of alienation in modern society is one of the main problems in the portrayal of human beings and fates. Thus, as is well-known, the meeting between Pierre Bezuhov, the honest and in many ways eccentric aristocrat, and the peasant, Platon Karatayev, directly precipitates a decisive change in Pierre's life, the consequences of which, following the defeat of Napoleon, are manifest above all in that in Petersburg he plays a leading role in the Decembrist circle. When he returns to his family and gives an account of himself, his wife, Natasha asks him the question: "Do you know what I'm thinking about? About Platon Karatayev. What would he have said? Would he have approve of you now?" Bezuhov ponders and says hesitantly: "Platon Karatayev? . . . He would not have understood . . . and yet, perhaps, he would . . . No he wouldn't have approved."[33] Here then Tolstoy sees clearly that the inner "ignorant perfection" of the common people is not sufficient to develop in man a positively effective and critical attitude towards the reform of his alienated society. In the process of socially concretizing the spontaneous and morally justified criticism of the common people a qualitative leap is required before this criticism can acquire a positive and effective human substance. This critique of the instinctual ideas of the common people is not an isolated "victory of realism" in Tolstoy. Decades later he shows in *Resurrection* that the turn from immorality to morality, i.e. to the individual good deed which the legal proceedings brought by Maslova against her first seducer, Prince Nekhlyudov induce in him, cannot awaken a genuine human re-birth in her (who, like many of

[33] Leo N. Tolstoy, *War and Peace*, Vol. 2, (Penguin Classics, Harmondsworth, Middlesex, 1969), p. 1396.

Solzhenitsyn's plebian heroes, holds a *Weltanschauung* which in content and form is very close to Platon Karatayev's). Only when, in direct consequence of Nekhlyudov's intervention she is brought together with exiled socialists on the way to Siberia can her human and moral regeneration really take place. In both cases, the critique of the *praxis* of plebeian ideology is not clearly expressed in terms of ideas but "merely" portrayed in a purely artistic manner. From the standpoint of literature, however, this is no insignificant matter. On the contrary, precisely in such cases a realm opens up, though admittedly one with fluid frontiers, in which great writers can qualitatively rise above the level of the merely significant, the extremely interesting, the deeply honest, etc.

An awareness of this level, a self-criticism of plebeianism at this profound social level, is as yet lacking in Solzhenitsyn's works. Of course this is very difficult to decide in individual cases; for example, Shulubin's social theories, which do not necessarily reveal the author's own views, come to mind. From the vantage point of great literature, however, it must be said that what is not realised in literary terms does not exist at all. Thus Shulubin's explanations remain elements of his psyche and do not become elements of an artistically critical picture of the period as is the case in the passages just quoted from Tolstoy. Nevertheless, it must not be said that Solzhenitsyn is wholly uncritical of the behaviour of his positive characters. This is evident at the conclusion of this novel. Kostoglotov never tires of repeating his wish to be released from the ward; he dreams again and again of an idyllic existence like that of his friends, the Kadmins, which he hopes finally to be able to enjoy at the close of his life; his approaches to the young doctor, Vera, and to the nurse, Sonya, are preparations for realizing such a longing. Now he is released and both women offer to let him stay in their houses for the transitional period. In high spirits he leaves the ward, and his first contacts with freedom indeed have an intoxicating effect on him. But by chance he does not find Vera at home; she has gone out. He wanders aimlessly into a department store, and the bustle that predominates there, the people's demand for commodities, disorient him completely. His desire to recover in the zoological garden also miscarries; he sees only captive, silent fellow-sufferers from his previous life. Without making another attempt to visit either of the two women, and inwardly completely broken, he climbs aboard the train to go "home".

Solzhenitsyn depicts this dénouement in a purely objective way. For that very reason, it seems to be the necessary outcome of Kostoglotov's position in life; it reveals that as soon as he ceases to be directly and polemically confronted with the power which has destroyed his life he becomes unable to continue with a life of his own. And since this inner collapse of the figure in whom the plebeian protest against the Stalinist period was not only most vigorously but also intellectually and morally best articulated forms the conclusion of the entire novel, it is difficult for the reader not to see in it a kind of artistic criticism of this attitude. For an artistic criticism, as opposed to a merely theoretical one, is not based on intellectual contradictions and inconsistencies. It is concerned instead to show how a certain attitude to life is realised in life itself, and how it can become the decisive factor in man's moral victory or defeat—also, whether this process of realization is a direct one, and if not, what are its intervening stages. Artistic criticism, then, reveals the individual human acts of human failure or success, but it is of the greatest importance that in so doing, it also reveals their social acts, while remaining exclusively on the level of the human and the individual. It is evident that without such a foundation the most sincere, honest and passionate subjective attitude remains inwardly flawed and incapable of even pure self-preservation.

We have already pointed out that the specific problematic

of the human self-realization allowed by modern bourgeois society found its most typical artistic form of expression in the various forms of humour. The human problematic of the political *citoyen* never included such problems, since his private role as a human being and public role as a citizen were then far too closely interconnected. But, as we have seen, the first and the most magnificent appearance of this modern literary genre, *Don Quixote*, attains an individuality never again achieved, an indivisible unity of objective humour and subjective grandeur, in that the human self-realization of the hero possesses a capacity for action which objectively has been made obsolete by historical development, but which subjectively is spiritually and morally unshakable. This unmediated subjective principle can, however, become an effective and active force compelling an inner recognition only if it can express an actual and permanently progressive motif permanently progressive, that is, from a human point of view, not necessarily from the point of view of the contemporary situation. The eccentricity of later, comic figures thus originated in an internal intertwining of the genuine and subjective spirit of opposition with its objective possibility of realization. In the case of Kostoglotov, precisely this subjective spirit of human self-defence is totally extinguished in the concluding scene; he collapses not outwardly but inwardly; he is not subdued by the factual power of the external world which had defeated him in exile, but by the transformation of his inwardness from a spirit of opposition to a state in which it is reduced to silence.

The first and most important aesthetic consequence of this is that the comic analysis (or sometimes, self-analysis) of eccentricity (which dominates much social criticism in the novel from Sterne to Raabe) here virtually disappears. Self-preservation which as a rule goes no further than the subject, and the ignorant perfections which appear now and then are presented as human ultimates. This diminishes and limits

Solzhenitsyn's otherwise so profound and pertinent artistic social criticism of an extremely important transitional period. In his analysis of the Stalin period at its height Solzhenitsyn rightly depicts the diversity of the ideological consequences of Stalinism. Nevertheless, objectively his whole critique confines itself in the last analysis to the damage done to the integrity of individual human beings. The humour of the realists just mentioned had the artistic function of bringing to light the additional facts, namely that in periods that give their honest critics and reformers no opportunity to act, such persons must succumb to a certain social and personal alienation. Humour is the artistic form which can express the duality of human nature, the simultaneous justification for and the powerlessness of such an attitude. The historical injustice of the world exposed to the full impact of critical passion need not be diminished by this, but is, on the contrary, magnified. The weakness of critics and reformers is seen to be a harmful consequence of such a repressive system. Such humour should be absent from Solzhenitsyn's portrayal of oppositional tendencies. This by no means destroys the truth and genuiness of his criticism, but only weakens his perspectives and indeed at times reduces them to the appearance of a lack of perspectives, inasmuch as the self-deliverance, the self-preservation of the best characters is enclosed in a purely abstract subjectivity, and inasmuch as the leap into action does not even appear as something that was once possible, even if problematic. For however indispensable the plebian factor is for any renewal of society—Lenin is the greatest example of this inseparable connection—any genuine transforming agency must transcend a mere self-conscious and ordinary plebian existence and consciousness. (Again Lenin is the great historical example of this.) It must not be forgotten, however, that literature began to advance in this direction not only in the works of the revolutionary democrats, but also in Tolstoy.

If, in consequence of this we conclude that Solzhenitsyn

criticizes the Stalinist period from a plebeian and not from a communist point of view, then this limiting judgement is not political in any primary and direct sense. Naturally this does not exclude indirect political interferences in the sense indicated above. However, if Solzhenitsyn does not develop in subsequent works, it will restrict his literary importance. For if we, as has been our practice throughout these reflections, hold with Ibsen and Chekhov to the view that the duty of the genuine writer is to concentrate on intensive questions and not on direct answers, we shall find everywhere questions of differing depth and significance the response to which ultimately determines literary stature. Our criticism is thus directed at the fundamental method of questioning on which Solzhenitsyn's work is based. It is· in no sense my wish to detract from his tremendous historical achievement of having proved himself a worthy successor to the important plebeian tradition which became one of the foundations of the greatness of Russian literature and which played a vital role in the first flowering of socialist realism. His works are undoubtedly the first and most important precursors of a new creative epoch.

For such a criticism—in both a positive and negative sense —to be exhaustive, it would have to be based on a comprehensive analysis and evaluation of the critical beginnings extant today. I cannot claim to have done this in these essays. I must confess this in a self-critical spirit, since not only, naturally enough, am I not familiar with the literature which doubtless exists but until now has remained "underground", but also I know much too little of what has been made public. This literature does, however, contain occasional instances of criticism of the Stalin era, some of which go beyond Solzhenitsyn's plebeian critical analysis. In order briefly to raise this problem, in order to point out the problematic of my own analysis, let us mention at least one work of this kind, the short novel of the Kirghizian poet, Chingiz Aitmatov

[English title: *Farewell, Gul'sazy*!].[34] In this novel we see the way in which the brutal bureaucratic manipulation of the Stalin system turned against those who, for all their sectarian prejudices, worked enthusiastically to bring about the socialist evolution, undaunted by the sacrifices demanded of them. We see how until their own tragic downfall, they were able to preserve their inner human commitment to the revolution in the midst of the destruction of their own existences. Their personal fates are thus not merely comic but rise to the level of tragedy and tragi-comedy. The existence of such novels must not be overlooked if one does not wish to lose sight of the overall development and its human basis and artistic and social perspectives. The importance of what has hitherto become available of Solzhenitsyn's life-work is not diminished if he is considered not as a solitary exception but as part of a larger current.

(1969)

[34] London, Hodder and Stoughton, 1970